COURAGEOUS JOY
THE JANET PERKINS STORY

Copyright © 2025 by Courageous Conversation®. All rights reserved. Published in the United States by Vision Publishing House.

Vision Publishing House
support@vision-publishinghouse.com
www.vision-publishinghouse.com

Compiled by Solomon Akumun
Edited by Nicole Queen
Cover photo by Duane Cramer
Cover design by Felix Frimpong

ISBN: 979-8-9933667-1-5 (print)
LCCN: 2025921997

This book is established to provide information and inspiration to all readers. It is designed with the understanding that the author is not engaged to render any psychological, legal, or any other kind of professional advice. The content is the sole expression of the author. The author is not liable for any physical, psychological, emotional, financial, or commercial damages, including, but not limited to special, incidental, consequential, or other damages. All readers are responsible for their own choices, actions, and results.

No part of this book may be reproduced in any form or by any electronic or mechanical means, including information storage and retrieval systems, without written permission from the author, except for the use of brief quotations in a book review. Reproduction of text in whole or part without the expressed written consent by the author is not permitted and is unlawful according to the 1976 U.S. Copyright Act.

This book is dedicated to my son, Glenn...

*To the memory of my mother, Helen Singleton, and my grandmother, Annie Ruth Johnson; and to all the Black women—those who came
before, those who are here now, and those yet to come.*

*You are the Black butterflies who, despite the turbulence
of this world, find the courage to create joy.*

ACKNOWLEDGMENTS

I thank the Creator for the gift of life and a life well lived, and my ancestors for their wisdom and guidance.

To my son, Glenn Singleton—thank you for encouraging me to share my story.

To my son-in-spirit, Solomon Akumun—thank you for helping me put these words into writing.

And finally, special thanks to my editor at Vision Publishing House, *Nicole Queen,* whose patience and expertise helped shape this work.

CONTENTS

Foreword Alice Jones	ix
Prologue	1
1. WHERE THE SUNFLOWER BLOOMED	7
The Fathers We Knew (And Didn't)	14
What The River Knows	26
Black Butterflies	37
Our People	45
2. THE ROAD WE TROD	63
3. BEFORE COURAGE HAD A NAME	75
Courage Was All She Had	94
The Softest Warrior	98
Wildflower	105
4. THE NAMES WE CARRY	121
A Whole New World	129
5. THE COURAGE TO CHOOSE YOU	141
6. IN SERVICE OF THE UNSEEN	153
7. A DIAMOND OF THE SUN	169
8. SEASONS AND LESSONS	189
No Regrets	190
Do Not Over-Plan	194
You Have to Act	200
Guard Your Integrity	205
Listen More, Talk Less	211
Say What You Mean & Mean What You Mean	216
Sankofa: Reach Back	221
Be Willing to Make Sacrifices	225

Be a Parent	229
One Day At A Time	237
Joy Like a River	240
About the Author	251

FOREWORD
ALICE JONES

Undoubtedly, walking beside my dearest friend, Janet Perkins, for more years than I can easily number—I count as one of the great blessings of my life. Our friendship was born out of destiny, not chance. It was such an ordinary place to meet: our neighborhood drugstore in Baltimore was where we met. We both worked there. I remember those days as if they were yesterday. How could I forget Janet's youthful and radiant presence, wearing that joyful smile that has never faded to this very day? In those earliest days, my soon-to-be "big Sister," Janet, carried a spirit of welcome. She was very clear—she took the job at the drugstore so she could take care of her son Glenn, who was barely six months old. Upon our meeting, Glenn was already Janet's pride and joy—the heartbeat of her life. And to this day, that bond between mother and son remains unbroken. My nephew Glenn adores Janet with the same fierce devotion I watched Janet pour into him more than sixty years ago. To watch them grow together has been to witness love in the purest form—a love that endures trials, defies hardships, and grows stronger with time.

Almost immediately, I sensed that Janet was the kind of person who would be in my life forever. It did not take long for us to begin building our relationship outside of our work together at the drugstore. I began visiting her Dolfield Avenue home often, especially on Sundays, where I was drawn not only to Janet's company but also to the warm embrace of her family. Miss Helen, Janet's fun-loving mother, made the best rolls, from scratch, in all of Baltimore—and I will confess that I went as much for those rolls as for anything else. But what kept me coming back on all other days was the atmosphere of love around that kitchen table, where laughter was easy and I was made to feel as if I had always belonged there.

Janet introduced me to my wonderful husband, Jay. For more than fifty incredible years that we have been together, I have been forever grateful. Jay has been my companion and source of joy and comfort through illness and good health. Her introduction alone would have been enough to cement Janet's place in my heart. Fortunately, Janet has never been a friend of convenience; she is a friend of covenant. She has been present in my highest moments and steadfast in my lowest.

Looking back on our colorful sisterhood, what strikes me most is Janet's unshakeable character. She embodies the fruits of the Spirit—kindness, love, patience, and generosity. She is quick to lend a hand, even quicker to open her heart. When we needed her, she was there without hesitation, no questions asked. And still, she is no saint carved from stone. Janet has her moods—her moments when she needs her space. But even in those moments, she teaches us the dignity of honoring one's boundaries. Janet is fully human. She is tender, fierce, loving, complex—and these are just some of the many characteristics and qualities that make her so remarkable.

Having countless incredible memories to share—trips we have taken together, evenings spent in quiet conversation, and the laughter that rolled out of her until it shook the room—what defines Janet more than any single memory is her courage. The title of her memoir, *Courageous Joy*, is perfect. From the day she chose to be Glenn's mother, I have known Janet to live a life of courage. I've known her to make decisions that were not always easy but always grounded in love. She has faced hardship with a fierce determination, never letting bitterness take root.

I recall a time when her marriage was troubled and her path was uncertain. Many would have folded under such a burden, but Janet endured. She kept her heart open. She kept on giving. She found her signature way to hold onto joy even in the midst of her deepest struggle. This is her gift: Janet can create joy where there seemingly is none, cling to it when it is fragile, and offer it freely to those around her.

Janet's story is both personal and universal. She is a Black woman in America, carrying a long history of burden and resilience. She successfully raised a Black son in a society that more often sees danger instead of promise in him. Janet worked, sacrificed, and stood firm while carrying the unspoken trauma that Black women have borne for generations. We have been uniquely called to lead our families, hold them together, and survive what others could not. Janet's life is a testimony to the strength of women who anchor their communities while carrying scars unseen.

But please do not think this is a story of suffering alone. Hers is a story of love—love for her son Glenn, love for her mother, Ms. Helen, and for her dearest Granny. Janet's story is one of love for an entire family, a community of friends, and love for the small joys of life—those rolls baked fresh on Sunday afternoon, the laughter that shakes the walls, and the friendships that span decades. This is the love that defines Janet and will pour off the pages of her memoir and into the hearts of all who read her beautiful story.

For readers who have not met the loving, courageous, and faithful Janet that I know, let this book serve as your invitation to step into her inner circle. Learn from her courage and be lifted by her joy. You will find in her words not only a chronicle of one fierce woman's life but also a mirror of your own resilience. Janet's story is Baltimore's story, America's story, and a Black woman's story that belongs to all of us who know what it is to suffer and still choose joy. Her laugh, her smile, and her unwavering spirit are gifts she gives to each of us on the pages that follow.

Janet is my friend, my sister, and my teacher. And now, through this memoir, she will be yours as well. Go right on and laugh with her, cry with her, and, most of all, be inspired by her. Because if there is one lesson I have carried from our many years together, it is this: love is the only legacy worth leaving, and joy—true joy—is an act of courage!

PROLOGUE
THE HOUSE THAT HOLDS YOU

I have observed, over the years, the slow erosion of the cords that once bound Black folk together. I have noticed it not just in the world around me but in my own family, my own life—at least from the time I first came to my own consciousness and to the consciousness of the reality of my world. This slow erasure has not been by chance; it has taken centuries of interruption, separation, exploitation, oppression, and suppression.

But there is a particular side of this violence of erasure that America does not name—or perhaps has chosen to name differently—because to name it as it should be named would be to take responsibility for it. It is not the kind of violence that we have come to know as the hallmark of America, the type that leaves blood on the sidewalks or bruises beneath the eye. This one is slower. Stealthier. It moves like a wildcat, with its claws retracted—walking only on the soft edges of its paws as it approaches its prey. It floats like smog rising out of a valley, invisible until you look around and realize you can no longer see the trees on the other side.

This is the violence of absence—of systems that have been designed through the years not to kill outright, but to wear us down, like water cutting through rock—until the Black woman begins to believe her struggle is natural and her exhaustion is her own fault. A slow, grinding force that breaks down the spirit. And it is here that my story begins, because this absence did not just shape a people; it shaped me. But perhaps the most devastating impact of this violence is single motherhood.

Particularly, the Black single mother in America—the burden and cruelty our foremothers carried and endured through the Middle Passage, and which is assigned to us from the moment we open our eyes to the sun. America loves to punish the Black woman for not having a man, even as it builds a prison for every man she might have had. It blames her for the family it broke. It shames her for the child she raises alone, even as it refuses to pay her a living wage, refuses to house her, and refuses to see her when she stands in line for help. She becomes both the mule and the villain, carrying generations on her back while being accused of raising them wrong. She wakes before the sun, prepares breakfast, kisses foreheads, rushes to work, and returns to find eviction notices or school suspensions waiting on the table. She is always late, always tired, always behind—because this country made it so.

You see, America has never forgiven the Black woman for being stronger than what it tried to break. And so it isolates her. Just as it has done since its interruption of Black life, it has turned the Black man into a ghost, made the system into a cage, and even turned her love into labor—and it is this labor that has become her fault.

This is the kind of violence we do not speak of because it hasn't screamed loud enough. Or maybe it has, but no one hears because it is drowned in the shouts of the constant fight for the liberation of our collective bodies, our souls. To be Black in this country is to be born into contradiction—pulled between strength and struggle, between survival and silence. And there is perhaps no circumstance where this contradiction is more evident than in family, the place we are taught to be the safest.

I was raised to believe that family is sacred—that it is the first place where we give love a name and a face, the tree we can always lean on when everything else around us lies in ruin, and where we can be sure to find resting solace when the world grows too loud or indifferent to the fears we are unable to name aloud. For Black folks in America, family is often our only consistent refuge, one of the few institutions still standing, albeit broken. But what they don't tell you—and perhaps what we are often too ashamed or too loyal to say—is that sometimes, the house that holds you is also the one that haunts you.

For me, America had already begun its plunder of my life even before I was born. My mother and her mother before her, suffered this violence—of teenage motherhood, of single motherhood—and it wasn't long before this violence found me too. I was born four months before the war ended—if it ever really ended. My biological father was off fighting at the frontlines. So not only did I feel the distant resounds of bombs and rifles and fighter jets through the tensed muscles of my mother's body, but I was also born into a warring world and inherited the trauma of the fear buried deep in her memory like shrapnel.

Perhaps the period in which I was born is the reason I value peace so much. And I know that peace is just the brief silence between battles, isn't it? A pause to reload. A breath before the next action.

They called it the "Good War" and said it was necessary and noble—to free the world and protect democracy. But when I look back, I wonder whose world was saved, whose democracy was defended, and at what cost. Because surely, it wasn't for people like my mother. And while the nation celebrated victory, my own story was only just beginning—born into a world where peace was promised but never delivered.

And now, at eighty, I still ask some of these questions. Why do we war? Is it for freedom? Or for flags stitched by empires with blood-threaded hands? Because if it is for freedom, then why weren't people like me and my parents free—free to move about, free to vote, free to live in the neighborhoods they wished to live in? Is it for justice? Then why were, and are, Black bodies still being shot at by the people who were meant to protect them, with no consequences? Or was it for profit? Or pride?

I have seen men die over land they cannot eat, over gods they cannot see, and over names they were given. We dress war in medals and memorials, in parades and poppies. But war—war is a butcher in uniform. It does not care who is right, only who is left. So I ask: did the war ever end, or just evolve? Did peace come, or just retreat into the shadows? These questions still echo in me today, even at eighty, as I look back over the battles I've witnessed and survived.

I was born in the year the world said *never again*. But I've lived long enough to see that promise broken—again and again. Maybe the real war is within us: in our thirst to conquer what we do not understand, in our fear of the other, and in our worship of power disguised as patriotism.

And yet, I still believe in the possibility of peace—not as a treaty signed in halls of stone, but as a choice made in hearts of flesh. A peace where memory, instead of haunting us, teaches us. Where Black boys can dance to music, not sirens. And it takes a certain kind of courage to live—with all the uncertainty, against all these odds—to dream, and to find joy in this land of dreamers.

1

WHERE THE SUNFLOWER BLOOMED

I do not remember the earliest years that followed my birth after the war ended—perhaps only faded glimpses of memories my mind can no longer fully recall. I lived with my grandmother, Annie Ruth, and my grandpa Johnson until I was about three years old. My mother, Mama Helen, married my adoptive father, John Singleton, when he returned from the war in 1948. He had—years earlier—moved to Baltimore from Columbia, South Carolina, at the age of five, after his parents, John and Irene Garner Singleton, passed away. I had just turned three when they got married. My formative years were shaped by my grandmother, my grandfather, and my mother—though my mother wasn't always around in those early years.

Granny Annie's story, I'd later come to see, was a depiction of the many other ways this country has broken the backs of those who built it—that long line of ancestral Black women who gave their pride, their wombs, their tears, their dignity, and ultimately, their lives. I see now that I come from women who knew how to make a way. Women who learned, too early, how to hide pain in the corners of their smiles. Who got pregnant too young, not out of recklessness, but because life was reckless with them. I come from girls turned mothers by fathers who had so much love to give but were never taught how to give it—no warmth to offer because they themselves were still in the cold, carrying only the rigid silence was passed down by a world that told us we could not cry. Not break. Could not be boys. Not be men. Only be soldiers for a war that had no medals for them.

Granny Annie was born in Warrenton, North Carolina. Her father—and this is where the story turns painful—kicked her out when she was just thirteen. Thirteen. A child herself, with a child in her arms—my Uncle Ransom. She had him too young, yes, but not without cause. This country had a way—and still does—of stealing Black girlhoods and leaving babies in their place.

It was 1921—two months after a mob of hateful White men had razed the Greenwood district of Tulsa—when her own father, Great-Grandpa Thomas Williams, looked past her innocence and told her to leave his house. Told her not to come back. But what cuts deeper than exile was the theft—he wouldn't let her take her baby. "You're not taking that boy," he said, and it wasn't out of concern, or love, or any sense of fatherly duty. He needed a pair of hands. The boy was labor. The land demanded sweat, and the Black body—even the body of his own grandson—was a tool in that economy of forty acres and a mule. With eyes lifted toward God and sorrow welling in her own, she left the house that should have been her refuge.

They told Ransom that she left him. That she walked away. That lie grew roots in him so deep it found its way into his obituary. And I remember saying to my brother, "Don't you give me no copy of that obituary. I already know what it says. And it's a damn lie." Because the wound was never hidden. I knew it as a girl. And yet somehow, not one of his six children ever asked the question. Not one of them dug into the soil of that version of the story they were told.

We say these things are forgotten, but that's not true. They are buried—by shame, by the same weight of oppression that, for four hundred years, has built a world where Black women can be cast out and still be blamed. That great interruption, with its visible hand of violence and its quiet engineering of erasure, of maintaining a narrative—the narrative that it is her fault. The Black woman's fault. It breaks the Black family at its root and then blames the fruit for not growing straight. It builds the cage, shuts the door, and hands us the key while whispering, "You *did this to yourselves.*"

What they call teenage pregnancy in our communities—what they moralize and parade as pathology—is often just the aftershock of a system that took everything: our history, our names, our men, and even our right to hope. Can you imagine? What they call the absence of fathers is often the presence of trauma, unspoken and unhealed, passed from man to man like a genetic inheritance of pain. Black men carry the scars of blame while the architects of this suffering walk free, wear suits, make laws, run banks, and teach our children to despise their own shadows.

And what of the women? Women like Aunt Polly—my grandmother's younger sister—who packed up her dignity and moved North, perhaps because she had a dream to chase, but certainly because the South had nothing left but dirt and ghosts. Women who became mothers and fathers, teachers and disciplinarians, lovers and fighters, because the men were gone—lynched, locked up, or lost in the war between their own pain and the world's cold indifference. Women who taught us how to set a table, how to iron our clothes, and how to survive a world that didn't want us to exist. Women who found the courage to live. Women like Granny Annie, on that cold morning when the fruit of her womb was torn away from her.

After the exile, my grandmother fled north—to Baltimore, to her younger sister, Aunt Polly, who years earlier had moved to what was then a haven for Black folks. She wasn't waiting around for the South to get gentle. She saw the place for what it was and long accepted that it was foolish to expect vipers not to strike their poison at the heels of those who threatened them. So she packed her pride, her lace tablecloths, and her dreams and left her father's farm behind. She never married, never had children—just carved out her life in the city like so many Black women who knew the cost of waiting for men to be men.

She lived on Madison Avenue—back when it was an old "white" part of town. And baby, Aunt Polly had style. She was the kind of woman who taught you how to sit, how to fold your napkin, and how to speak without raising your voice. She was an Eastern Star, an Elk—part of those Black institutions that held dignity for us when America offered none.

She wore white—always white. Perhaps it was for her order. Maybe for work. I don't know. But I remember those clothes were always sent out to be cleaned, not washed by hand. She had things delivered, and that meant something back then. That meant she had money—not a lot, but enough to hold her head high.

Her place was an efficiency—small but deliberate. Everything was just so on point. Lace on the tables, not too expensive, but they were hers. And on weekends, when her Star sisters came over, I'd be there too, in the living room, just a few steps from the laughter. They poured their tea from fine porcelain kettles. And they talked. Lord, they talked. It was from Aunt Polly that I learned the importance of sisterhood—bonds built from a deliberate choosing of familial community. And sometimes, an unexpected blessing from the universe, an ancestor finding us again.

And Great-Grandpa Williams—my grandmother's father—I never met him. But his shadow was long. He ruled with that old Southern iron hand. And Aunt Martha, one of his daughters, stayed. Married, maybe. Had twelve or thirteen children. She stayed on that land, raised her house on it, and found pride in it. And while that land was inheritance, it was also chains. And for Granny Annie, it was a land of no return.

Some summers I went to visit and stayed with Aunt Martha. My brother Wesley wouldn't go—he was a city boy through and through. Didn't like the countryside one bit. That place—it was Black richness. Not richness in the sense of money, but land and the goodness of nature's bounty. Collards, cabbage, and corn—they grew out of the ground like a birthright. To a child born in the city, it seemed unusual, because food was supposed to be on the shelves, not on stalks and vines.

Chickens—Lord, the chickens. They strolled the yard like they owned it, constantly pecking the earth for whatever they desired: grains, stones, grass, or worms. And when the sun god rested his lamp behind the mountains of the west, they slept wherever they felt comfortable—in the coop, the trees, or simply under shrubs. I still remember the day Aunt Martha killed one in front of me. Twisted its neck and put it in my hands while it was still warm. Perhaps her way of saying, "You will know life, and you will know death. And you will not fear either." And later, when I had a bite of it after she had prepared it, I wondered if it was the same thing we ate back in Baltimore.

That moment stayed with me—a child's first lesson in life and death. Granny Annie's story may be sad for many people, but her story is just another obscure side of America's story. The Black story. And it is, unfortunately, all too familiar to many. The lie of abandonment and the myth of dysfunction—all serving the same god: white supremacy. A god that demands Black sacrifice without end and then turns its face when we bleed.

My grandmother, my great-aunts, even my own biological father—they were not broken people. They were people broken by a system. And it is easier for America to believe we are the architects of our own ruin than to face the truth—that the house, this union, was built to collapse on top of us. After all, it has always stood on our bent backs.

And I share her story not to dwell in sorrow, nor to justify, but to testify. To remind the world, and ourselves, that our families, even in fragments, were full of love. That our mothers did the best they could with the pieces they were given. That our fathers—many of them—were taken from us by systems too cruel to be named. That the cycle is not ours. The cycle is theirs. But the healing? That belongs to us. And it began with women like my grandmother—cast out, broken, but never erased.

THE FATHERS WE KNEW (AND DIDN'T)

I lived with my grandparents until I was three. My world was still new and tender, and I didn't yet have the words for the things I was feeling—only the difference between quiet and tension, peace and pretending. And even as a child, I could read between the lines. I knew when Granny was happy with me or when Grandpa was angry at something I had done.

My grandmother worked for a wealthy Jewish family on the other side of town—the Walperts. Mrs. Walpert, the matriarch, had polio. I didn't really understand what that meant at the time—only that her legs didn't work the way mine did, and she moved slowly, with a kind of grace that looked painful. A grimace made me wonder why her face was always the way it was. Granny was her caretaker. She helped her dress, helped her bathe, and helped her feel like a woman again. It was delicate work, sacred work. And I didn't realize it then, but it was a kind of service that wasn't just about the pay she received. It was about dignity—keeping someone else's world intact while your own teetered on the edge. I knew this years later, when I would care for her and my own mother in the same way.

On weekends, I'd go with my grandmother to the Walperts' house. She never said it out loud, but I know now that she didn't like leaving me alone with my grandfather. He was a good man in the way Black men of his generation were expected to be good—hardworking, proud, and emotionally distant. He laid concrete by day and laid up with the bottle by night. He'd come home smelling of sweat and liquor, take off his boots, and collapse into bed with little more than a grunt. My grandmother used to shake her head and say, "I can always count on him bringing that stinky alcohol home and going right to bed." She said it with a little laugh—the kind that carried more resignation than humor.

The Walpert house was different. It was quiet—almost too quiet. They spoke in hushed tones; everything was always on the verge of a library whisper. There were books in every room and photographs in gold frames. They had tea in porcelain cups and didn't shout across rooms. Nobody ever raised a hand. Nobody ever raised their voice. For a little Black girl raised on call-and-response and the clatter of cast-iron skillets, it felt like another world. And yet, even as a child, I sensed something familiar beneath the differences.

Mrs. Walpert's hands trembled sometimes when she tried to button her blouse. I'd sit on the floor watching my grandmother gently steady her wrists. There was a kind of unspoken tenderness between them—not quite friendship or family, but more than duty. It were two women, two mothers, who saw each other.

I started to notice the loneliness in the Walpert house. Despite the fancy rugs and velvet chairs, there was a kind of sadness that hovered. The openness that existed in our little neighborhood was missing here. Neighbors didn't yell from across the street to check in with each other. No unexpected visitors dropping by the porch to "check in on y'all." No hearty chatter on weekends with smoke rising from barbecue grills around the corner. Just an old couple caught up in a world they had perhaps helped create, where isolation was prized over community. And so, even though the chaos in our house was loud, it was the love that put everything in its place.

When I turned three, my mother married John Singleton. I was born in that tender place between war and awakening, and I remember those early years only with a clarity that tastes like copper and childhood dust. Memory, in our people, isn't just a picture show; it is a reeling sound of music and aromas over the years—the songs our parents sang and listened to, the food our grandparents cooked. A spoon clinking against a pot, a voice humming something halfway between gospel and mourning. Memory, for us, is whose music ruled the airwaves that year and which civil rights leader threatened the White world the most at the time.

I remember the way the air shifted when he came into our lives. He didn't walk so much as claim space. John Singleton. Daddy. That's what I called him, and what he insisted I call him. "Ain't no 'step' in love," he once told me as he tightened my shoes before church. And I believed him, because children believe things their hearts long to hear. He adopted me in name, in gesture, and in every way that mattered in the eyes of law and family. But love, in the world

I was born into, always had a catch—a hidden bruise you didn't feel until later.

What I didn't know then—what my little-girl self was too busy skipping past—was that Daddy, for all his warmth and protectiveness, was also a man made of corners. He loved me, yes. but his love carried conditions sewn into it like tight seams. He wanted me to be his—his fresh start, unblemished by the bloodline of another man. So he erased from my early consciousness the presence of my biological father—the man who gave me my nose, my hands, and the bend in my walk I didn't inherit from Mama.

My mother never spoke of my father until I was ten years old. I remember that evening like the smell of rain on summer dust. I was in the tub, my small brown body surrounded by warm water and the gentle swoosh of silence. She sat beside the tub, like she always did when she gave me a bath, but this time her eyes carried an unusual kind of weight. "There's something I want to tell you," she said.

Now, a child may not yet know the language of sorrow, but she knows how it feels. And I felt it then, in the hushed tremor of her voice and the slow, deliberate way her hand moved over my wet curls. I looked up at her, my little eyes curious and waiting.

She took a deep breath and heaved a sigh that felt more like a tornado than an exhale. And in a tone both soft and solemn, she said, "Daddy—John Singleton—is not your real father." There was another name, one I had never heard in our home before: James Moss. And he lived in New York.

This was, of course, a transfiguration. A truth I'd long held was melting right before me. I did not cry, nor did I rage. Because children, God bless them, often accept the unimaginable as simply new. And as I grew into myself, I held no bitterness for the man who raised me. My mother, in her wisdom, advised me not to get angry with him, because it was all something John had decided. She let me write to James Moss, and he would write back through his brother, my uncle Freddie.

My biological father's story is another tale of how this country has systematically chipped away at the very foundation of Black familyhood—woven not out of deliberate choices but from the long, ragged threads of a nation whose very history has been the commodification of Black bodies, the capitalization of war, and a people still unwilling to recognize the full humanity of Black life.

He was born in 1923 in Harrisburg, Pennsylvania, where he spent the formative years of his life before moving down to Baltimore. When he met Mama, he was a military policeman—"military police," as we called them. A Black man in uniform at a time when the nation he served did not serve him. He went off to war like so many of our men—shoulders squared, chest proud, heart tethered to the promise of coming home to what was his: his own family. My mother was already pregnant with me when he left. But war has a way of unmaking things. It doesn't just take lives—it rearranges time, rearranges love, and sometimes, by the time you come back—if you make it back at all—what you left behind has already learned how to live without you.

After the war, he didn't return until late 1945 or '46. When he eventually stepped back onto American soil, my mother had already met John Singleton, and they were married. The door had closed. He'd later say to me, "I never had my heart broken like that." And I believed him—and still do. Because there's a special kind of heartbreak that comes from being forgotten by the ones whose photo in your breast pocket kept you going while fighting for a country that barely remembers your name.

During the war, when he was transporting Japanese prisoners through Fort Meade, Maryland, he'd load up the trunk of the vehicle before making his drop-offs. He always routed himself through the block on Appleton Street, where we lived at the time. He said he needed to see me, even if from a distance. My grandmother would lift me up to the window—a little girl too young to understand the significance of uniforms or separation or what was going on—and I'd wave. That was our ritual.

The prisoners—men he was charged with guarding—would call out to me in broken English. "My little princess," they'd manage to say with the little English they could muster, the same way my father used to call me. That's how my nickname at the time, *Little Princess*, came about. It may seem strange, but tenderness has a way of slipping into even the most militarized moments. In the middle of war, in uniforms and chains, these men still recognized something innocent, something worth protecting. These men, "enemies of the state," stripped of their power, still saw me as something precious. My father said, "Your grandmother taught you well," because I always waved and smiled. And those prisoners, riding past my childhood, would lift their hands and greet me like I was something holy. A royal offspring. A high priestess. That window was a stage for both heartbreak and hope—two sides of history. One side would someday fight for the freedom of the oppressed. The other side, well, some never made it out alive.

But that was just one window. Behind it was a house like many others—Black families held together by women and prayer. And that war, like most wars, left scars deeper than the eye could see. The Second World War took more than time from our men. It took connection. It took fathers from daughters. It took husbands from wives and gave them back broken, haunted, or sometimes not at all.

Black men went to Europe and the Pacific, fighting tyranny abroad while segregation and lynching ruled the streets at home. They returned to families that had been forced to move on, to women who had to learn how to survive without them, and to children who grew up thinking "Daddy" was a letter in a box or a story told at bedtime. For some of them, the hardest part wasn't the battlefield—it was the emptiness that greeted them afterward. And Black women—my mother, my grandmother—they had to become everything.

My father lost a family. And though I knew him later in life—through telephone calls and the long, soundless encouragement—it was always laced with the unspoken: the years that got away, the what-ifs and almosts, the regrets, and the faint resentment at the system that made it so.

We spent many years talking over the phone. He lived in New York and never came back to Baltimore after he left. He vowed he wouldn't return when he found out my mother had married John Singleton. He said he'd only come back if it was to get something important, but he had a brother in Washington, D.C.—Uncle Freddie—who handled things for him. While working in New York, he met and married Josephine Moore in 1959, and in 1965 they moved to Binghamton, New York, where they settled permanently.

But children aren't saints—we stumble, we test, and we spit out the fruits we once begged for. And so, while coming to terms with the new knowledge that Daddy—the one I grew up with—was my adoptive father, I did act up a bit afterward.

One evening, I was outside talking to my friend Phyllis, and I was expressing some frustration with having to deal with Daddy's strict rules, which seemed to be blended into the very paint that lined the walls of our house, and I said something along the lines of, "He isn't even my father! "

Daddy overheard me and called me into the house to sit in the kitchen with him and my mother. I was being a typical petulant teenager, you know. I had just started junior high school and was feeling a bit rebellious. That evening, he expressed disappointment in my actions, and we had a conversation about it. Mom scolded me and told me it was disrespectful to say that. Of course, as a child, it didn't make sense to me what the big deal was, but as I grew older, I realized just how much I had disrespected him that day. We give love, and we expect a certain measure of it back. And Lord knows Black men have received very little of that. Black fathers, still scarred.

I always felt special, especially being one of the few Black kids among a lot of Jewish children at school. I sat in Latin class, mastering just enough to pass and get out of there. Looking back, it's hilarious—I thought I might want to be a doctor, and I figured I might need Latin to write prescriptions. What a crazy thought! But my mother supported whatever I thought I wanted to be.

With time, I realized there was no anger toward either of my fathers. The way my mother framed it made room for grace, which made it easier for me to grasp. She taught me that my parents were more like guides in my life, not possessors. One of my favorite authors, Khalil Gibran, talks about how children are loaned to you, not owned, and that's how I now see my relationship with my parents. There were no heavy restrictions—just enough to let me explore and learn from my mistakes. She gave me room to try, to fail, and to try again. And at the time, there was no dictation by White men through "legislation" about how Black men could raise their sons. So, a little spanking here and there, a little cracking of the switch, ensured that we knew what actions carried consequences and which carried applause. Consequences were clear; love was constant. My mother and I would talk a lot about this—especially how Wesley, my immediate younger sibling, was the wild one. She knew it too! It was all part of our family dynamic, and we embraced it.

My father used to say that it broke his heart when my mother, in his words, "with her frisky self," decided to marry John Singleton. He told me, "That man wouldn't let me have anything to do with you." So he had to send his brother—Uncle Freddie. I remember Uncle Freddie coming to get me every weekend after I had moved in with my mother and John. He was the only man Daddy would allow me to spend time with. Uncle Freddie would take me to Granny Annie's house, and they treated me like royalty—cookies, milk, anything I wanted. They spoiled me like the little princess I was.

Daddy used to remind me of that when I got older, especially when I started asking questions about why he had kept my biological father away for so long. He really had no good reason, other than wanting to protect me in his own way. My biological father didn't reappear in my life until I was about to leave middle school and head to high school. That's when he put his foot down and demanded some time with me. I spent that summer with him in Brooklyn. The second time I would see him again, I was a mother.

I learned early that love can be present in more than one place and still leave a hollow. Fathers can be near and far at once. What I kept was what they each tried to give me: protection, pride, and a name to answer to. What I lost lived in the pauses. The next lessons would come the hard way.

My biological father, James Moss

WHAT THE RIVER KNOWS

Childhood innocence is bliss, but the reality of growing up—of becoming conscious, especially as a young Black girl—is different, and perhaps even more scathing, in these United States of America. I was fortunate to be raised by a woman who helped me keep my shoulders high—a mother who spoke positivity over my life every chance she got. "I know you're smarter than that," she'd say when I'd do the dumbest thing. It wasn't constant praise—it was more like guidance. I had to prove myself through my actions. Independence wasn't something that was handed to us; we earned it as we lived. Life was simple, but there was a lot of pride in the things we did, especially within the family. We took care of each other, learned from each other, and valued what we had.

When I was five, my mother had to homeschool me after I developed rheumatic fever—or rheumatism, as it was called then—the kind that steals the strength from your limbs and sends fear through every corner of a parent's body. I couldn't walk for a while, so I missed the entire first grade. She wasn't a teacher, at least not by the professional standards of the colonial world, but she was mine. She turned the house into a classroom. The kitchen table became a desk, and even the porch became a citadel of learning. Perhaps it was the dedicated attention, or the informal setting—the familiarity of the space—that made learning more assimilable. I grasped concepts better than when I had to sit in a classroom.

When I returned to school the following year, the teachers took one look at me and said, "She's been out, but we need to test her. Let's see where she belongs." And when the results came back, the surprised teachers said, "She can skip third and fourth." But Mama said no. She didn't think I was mature enough. That's the thing about Black mothers—they know that brilliance without grounding can become a burden.

I watched the adults around me fight for many years, demanding some of the freedoms other people enjoyed simply for having a different shade of skin. These were the days of the movement. I watched them contort, pass, aspire to be, and present themselves as capable too. They changed the way they spoke and the way they dressed because they had been told their way of life, their culture, was below the "standard." In retrospect, I see how different things are now, especially in how Black culture has evolved. There's a lot of freedom today, which is good, but I sometimes wonder how we've lost some of the values that held us together back then. Oh yes—integration. White education.

We grew up with respect—respect for family, for the elders, for learning, and for the ancestors that came before us. In our fight, we lost some parts of us. The parts that make us truly human. Community. Because those parts simply cannot exist within the construction of pale culture. Empathy. Because to be White is to not care. To divide. To oppress. To mind your damn business.

I think of my grandfather, Thomas Johnson. He, like the men he hung out with at the liquor store, had seen enough of this country to know there was very little hope for the sons after them. Hands browned by time, and a stare that could quiet a grown man's nonsense from across the room. He didn't speak often, but when he did, his words came out carved, like they were shaped by the vestiges of ancestral wisdom.

I was five when I first understood that Poppa walked differently when he left the porch. Inside the house, his body was light, soft even—like a Sunday morning prayer—but out there, in the world where White men held the sky between their fingers, he became smaller. A hat pulled low, a "yes sir" on the tongue, and eyes always watching, but never staring too long. He'd work hard all day, then go out with the boys to drink. He'd come home, sleep it off, and repeat the cycle. But that was America in the '50s—a land too proud to admit its sins and too drunk on its own freedom to care who it crushed beneath its boots. Men like Johnson knew that. They wore their dignity like a hidden lining, stitched beneath their coats. They learned how to survive without being seen, how to provide without being praised, and how to hold their anger like a full cup—steady, still—when everything around them tried to tip it over.

He went out one evening to drink with the other men, as he usually did, only this time he never returned home. The next day, his body was found on the street. My grandmother tried to explain it to me as best she could. She said Grandpa had gone to be with the Lord. That was my first experience with death. Reality, even to a child, comes naked. I was too young to know grief, to understand what it meant when someone died—the permanence of their absence. *Gone*. A word I had heard before when someone left a room or when the train pulled away from the station. But this was different. This *gone* felt too permanent.

Before that, I believed everything could return—Mama when she went to work, Christmas when we took down the last decoration. But when he left, I realized that some absences stay. The next time was Daddy's mother, who lived with us until she passed, just after my mother had my brother Irvin—and this I remember more clearly.

My little brother Irvin was such a beautiful boy. But beautiful things don't always last. It was the summer of 1959 —I remember it the way a ghost remembers a life. The edges of the moment are worn and frayed, but the feeling still lingers. I was fourteen and Wesley was eleven when Irvin passed at the unripe age of eight. We'd later find out that his cause of death was an aneurysm.

When Irvin was born, I discovered a side of me I didn't know was there—the part of me that was my mother. Irvin was my little brother. Not in the way Wesley was, for Wesley and I sometimes forgot who the older one was. But Irvin? He was mine. My very own little brother. And I took so much care of him, the way a hen takes care of its eggs.

My heart broke a thousand times the morning he passed. Irvin wasn't supposed to go first. He was the baby. He had a future like fire—bright, wild, untamed. Did he annoy me sometimes? Sure. But he had that thing, that thing some Black boys have—a smile that made the world forget, if only for a second, the danger it had assigned to their skin. He laughed like he invented the sound. He followed me everywhere—down the hall, into Mama's room, across the street. He was my little shadow. But brighter. Too bright for this world, maybe.

When my baby brother Irvin arrived, I wasn't ready for how much I'd love him. I was older—old enough to understand what it meant to protect. He was small, soft, and all knees and elbows and questions. And then one morning, he didn't wake up.

Losing him taught me that grief doesn't just take the person—it rearranges the ones who remain. But it was Wesley who suffered the most. The grief of losing a sibling is never just about their death but also the stories that won't be told now. The seat that will stay empty at dinner or Christmas. The sound of your own voice calling their name in a room they no longer occupy. And for Wesley, it was the empty space on the other side of the bed they shared that would never feel the same—haunted by the permanence of his absence. They shared a bed, and Wesley didn't realize at the time that Irvin wasn't just in a coma beside him, as he had been told that morning when he woke up to find Irvin still and motionless.

I imagine the sun had risen without apology—slanting in through the blinds, painting gold strokes across the floor, touching Wesley's eyelids with that familiar heat that signals the break of a new day. He rolled over instinctively, expecting to hear the soft snore or feel the push of Irvin's knees against his back. But the bed was still. Perhaps too still. He called his name. Once. Twice. Then he touched him. There are moments that change everything in a person's life. This was his. Irvin was cold. His lips parted just slightly. His eyes shut like sleep. But his chest did not rise.

His breath had left without sound, without struggle, and without signaling a warning. He had passed on. That realization, when it came later, was so traumatic for Wesley that he had to receive psychiatric treatment for a couple of years, from around the time he was eleven until he was thirteen or fourteen. Grief became his new bedmate. It followed him into school, into sleep, and into the solitary moments when someone said Irvin's name like it hadn't been buried. He blamed himself—of course he did. What else does a child do when the one person who looked at him like he was invincible died without warning, without reaching out?

He stopped sleeping well. Stopped talking much. He would lie in bed, eyes wide open, afraid to turn over. Afraid to wake again to another absence. It was only much later, when Wesley was diagnosed with terminal cancer, that we talked about the events of those old days.

And Mom? She disappeared into grief. She returned that day from University Hospital—where Irvin had been taken—a stranger. Her eyes empty, her voice lost. I was sitting out on the porch when she arrived, but she did not notice me, almost like I was invisible. She walked past me into the living room, wordless. For days she sat unmoving, unknowing of her children, not tending even to little Wesley. Reality pressed down on her until she nearly buckled, until madness itself seemed kinder than truth.

Madness seemed a mercy then. Madness looked like an open window in a house filled with smoke. She teetered at the edge of that window for days, and we—children still—watched, powerless to pull her back. We did not know it then, but that was the first time she went into a crisis. The loss left a hollow in the house that nothing could fill. Her body sat in the chair, but her spirit was gone to a place no one could follow. I saw my mother—the woman I had come to see as the strongest human God ever created—broken into shards my little heart could not gather together. She had always been proud, but now she leaned to the side, as though an unseen hand was shoving her, daring her to fall.

Daddy bore it the way men were taught to bear things—jaw tight, back straight, silence stitched across the mouth. He moved through the days like a soldier marching on blistered feet—not stopping, not faltering, just pressing forward, because to stand still would be to fall. He did not cry in front of us—if he did. Men of his making were not allowed that release. Instead, he folded his grief into work shirts and heavy shoes. He "took it as a man," they would have said—with a stride that was painful but graceful. And I watched him, learning what it meant to walk through sorrow without stumbling, even when the weight bowed his shoulders.

He said little, but the silence that clung to him was different from Mama's—it was not emptiness, but endurance. He was determined to keep us moving, to not let Irvin's absence unmake what remained. And so we moved on.

But life is a trickster, and you never know what it has up its sleeves. Ten years later, on exactly the day Irvin was born—and two years after he passed—Wendell was born, as if the Almighty Himself meant to replace sorrow with new breath. June 12th—death and birth stitched together across a decade. I was sixteen when Wendell came. Wesley, thirteen. It was a shock—or just a surprise—to everyone.

The air in our home was already heavy, for Mama had begun to carry her own storms. And his arrival broke whatever was left of the veil that shielded her sanity. A week after he was born, she went into her second crisis. This time, it consumed her completely. She left the house like the day she was born—unclothed—and wandered the streets, wild and untethered. This continued for days until Daddy had her committed to Crownsville State Hospital—a psychiatric hospital located in Crownsville, Maryland, that opened in 1911 as the third asylum in the United States to treat African American mental patients. The place was known for its harsh conditions, overcrowding, and use of experimental treatments, finding its place in history for its role in the racial segregation of mental health care in America.

They gave her shock treatments that hollowed her voice and dimmed her light. I hated it. She came home a quieter woman, emptied of her usual talk, like a songbird that had forgotten its tune. At the time, they diagnosed her with schizophrenia—as they did for nearly every Black person who presented with a mental health condition. For three months she was gone, and I—still a girl myself—became Wendell's mother. School in the morning, diapers and bottles in the evening, with Granny helping where she could.

When the responsibilities became too much for me to bear alone, Granny moved in to help. She did it so I wouldn't have to quit my job and become a full-time second mother to him. But one day, Daddy decided he didn't need her help anymore, so he put her out. Just like that. Shoved her out as he hurled curses at her. She fell hard, rolled off the steps, then picked herself up with more dignity than he could ever hold in his hands. She straightened her skirt and said, "Thank you very much," like a queen dismissing her court. And she never came back.

She'd later move in with me after I moved out. And it's funny how life loops back around. She lived with me for the last six years of her life. I lived with her for the first six years of mine.

With my brothers, Wesley and Irvin

BLACK BUTTERFLIES

Even the grief of death does not prepare you for the reality of being a Black child in America. Death may sometimes look like a relief, a saving grace. I learned early that living will break you. A law here. A look there. A sign at the store. A missed opportunity. A hand clutching a purse at the mere sight of your shadow. A red-and-blue siren behind you.

I grew up in segregated America. And—as hard as it is for me to say—Lord knows a part of it protected and protects Black bodies and spirits, even as it confined us and limited our access to resources and the full promise of the Union. We lived on Appleton Street, a small street made up of several rowhouses that branched off Riggs Avenue, separated briefly by a railway before connecting to Route 40.

My early schooling was a microcosm of a Black world, a segregated sanctuary where the faces mirrored my own, and the voices that guided us—from the principal's office to the classroom's chalk dust—were undeniably, proudly Black. It was an all-Black elementary school. The air in those classrooms was thick with a particular kind of aspiration, propelled largely by an army of Black men and women—teachers, mentors, custodians of our intellectual awakening. They were, almost without exception, highly educated, their knowledge a balm and a weapon against the systemic forces that sought to diminish us. They were the architects of our burgeoning minds, instilling not just arithmetic and grammar but also a sense of self-worth in a world that often sought to deny it.

It was mostly women who taught us, and they were highly qualified. Yet even within this sanctuary, the shadow of a larger, more insidious reality loomed. We also had boys in the school who weren't going to succeed academically but were talented with their hands—a tactile brilliance that defied the conventional metrics of academic success: electronic repairs, auto mechanics, and creative vocations. They were, in their own way, brilliant, but their brilliance was often deemed unsuitable for the regimented halls of traditional learning.

The reasons were complex, tied to the treacherous tendrils of the environment—the ghettos, as they were called—to the "behaviors they picked up at home." But even these behaviors, deemed "inappropriate for school," were often the unacknowledged scars of a society that had already, long before they stepped into a classroom, decided their fate. These boys were shunted into vocational programs, separated from the girls—a quiet act of triage that, while perhaps well-intentioned on the surface, reflected a deeper, more troubling truth: even within our own segregated spaces, the resonance of societal prejudice sorted our futures before we ever took our seats.

Wesley and I walked everywhere like Hansel and Gretel. We walked two miles to school every day from kindergarten through sixth grade, and we'd even walk home for lunch because we had an hour break. It was a tight-knit community, and we often walked long distances on weekends too—to the movies, to the ice cream parlor, or to visit family friends.

I think there's a peculiar truth that often gets lost in the rightful condemnation of segregation's brutal injustices: for those of us who grew up within its enforced boundaries, there was, paradoxically, a kind of unexpected grace—like a protective cocoon woven from the ragged threads of our own kind. It's a sentiment difficult to articulate without inviting misunderstanding, for no one sane would argue for the return of such an oppressive system. Yet to deny the unique strengths and solidarities forged within those Black communities would be to erase a vital part of our history.

The schools were an extension of our homes, filled with Black principals and Black teachers who understood our experiences, our dreams, our language, and the subtle nuances of our upbringing in a way no outsider ever could. They saw us not as exceptions but as the rule. They nurtured us with a firm hand and an unwavering belief in our potential, instilling in us a sense of belonging and capability that went beyond the limited horizons America had imposed on us This was a tight-knit community, where neighbors were family and the streets our playgrounds.

I like to think of my Granny, Annie Ruth Johnson, as a woman carved from oak and sunshine. I'm talking midday sun on the equator, with the world's knowledge etched into the deep knowing lines around her eyes. She understood the tricky dance of light and shadow—the way hope could be a cruel mirage and how often, for us, reality arrived unvarnished, sharp as a switchblade. She knew it, and so, like the generations of Black daughters who had come before her and those who would follow, I, too, had to know it.

One afternoon, the kind where the sun felt like a benediction on your shoulders—like the last person to reach Hades forgot to close the gates behind—she took my hand (how I loved holding Granny's hand when we walked) and led me downtown. Our destination that day was Stewart's Department Store. SDS was on the "Whiter" side of the city. It loomed, a multi-storied colossus of commerce, its plate-glass windows reflecting the bustling street, promising a world of silk and tweed and sparkling trinkets. To my eight-year-old eyes, it was a palace, a shimmering temple of possibility.

This was to be my first time shopping at Stewart's, but it was also going to be my first lesson on race relations in America. Before we even reached its gleaming glass doors, Granny's voice—soft yet firm as river stone—stopped me.

"Now, baby," she began, with that familiar look she had whenever she wanted you to know this was serious business, "we're going in there, and we're going to look. We are going to see all the pretty things. But there's something you have to understand." She paused, and I felt the weight of her words before they fully formed. "We can shop here, you hear me? We can spend our money. But we can't try nothing on. Not a single thing."

First came a ripple of confusion, then a prickle of unease beneath my skin. Why? The question was a tiny, insistent bird trying to escape my throat.

"Because, child," she explained, the words coming out with the tense dignity of a judge rendering a verdict, "it's against the law for us. Us colored folk. We aren't allowed to put the clothes on our skin."

Those words sank heavy—not that I understood them fully at eight years old, but I could feel the difficulty with which they rolled out of her voice. I could not make sense of it, no matter how much I tried. What was this violation I was experiencing? It was my first lesson that in America, the same dollar could buy you a dress but not the right to know if it fit.

Illegal. The word hung in the air, a thick, palpable thing. It wasn't about size, or money, or whether something would look good. It was about skin. My skin. Our skin. The very color that made me me and that made her her was a barrier—an invisible wall raised around the softest, simplest, yet most intimate act of something as ordinary as choosing a garment.

When we stepped inside, the air was cool and the ambiance hushed. The large hall was lulled by slow jazz music from speakers in the ceiling, perfumed with the scent of new fabric and polished wood. My grandmother, ever the picture of radiant grace, was a woman who adored hats. We moved through the ground floor, a dazzling array of accessories spread before us: mountains of gloves, shimmering scarves, sleek pocketbooks, and, most captivatingly, a veritable garden of hats—wide-brimmed, cloche, feathered, and veiled. My eyes, wide with wonder, darted from one beautiful thing to another.

Her instructions still rang in my head like a church bell tolling the Angelus at midday: *Do not touch anything.* If I saw something that captured my fancy, I could only point. My small finger, trembling slightly, would extend—a still gesture of desire across a chasm of unspoken rules. It was like standing before a bountiful feast and being told you could look, you could want, but you could not taste. And yes, like everything else to do with racism, it never made sense. Yet it was the initial shard of awareness, piercing the innocent veil of childhood, showing me that the world outside our warm, Black neighborhood had a different set of rules—harsh rules—written in the inconspicuous ink of prejudice.

It was, for me, the first violence of seeing the world for what it was. These were the years when being Black in America meant knowing your place, as they used to say. The '50s. It was a time of colored-only water fountains, segregated schools, and back-of-the-bus seating. It was a time when flying meant getting your wings clipped—and not flying at all meant dying in your cocoon.

It wasn't merely a matter of geography, a visible line drawn in the sand dictating where your feet could tread and where they could not. Oh no—it was far deeper, snaking into the very wellspring of a child's imagination, dictating what you could and couldn't dream. The entire system, with its labyrinthine rules and unspoken threats, was meticulously designed to keep you in your "place"—a designated, circumscribed space that encompassed not just your physical body but your mind and, most tragically, your very spirit. Our soul. The soul of Black folks.

Our schools were separate, a stark reality I lived daily, but they were by no stretch of the imagination equal. The buildings themselves told vivid tales of neglect: worn floorboards, chipped paint, and textbooks handed down from white schools—sometimes with pages missing or lessons outdated. Yet within those walls, our Black teachers, despite the meager resources, performed daily miracles—stretching every penny, unfolding the ears of those tattered maps, and igniting a fire of knowledge within us. They understood the stakes—the monumental task of preparing us for a world that simultaneously demanded excellence and denied opportunity.

Beyond the formal structures was another terrifying ballet of unspoken rules that governed our every interaction with the wind of the white world. These were the rules that hung in the clouds, passed down through generations of knowing glances and quiet warnings. "Don't look a white person in the eye too long," my grandmother would caution. "It's disrespectful."

"Disrespectful," I would later come to understand, was a euphemism for "dangerous." And for God's sake, "don't talk back." This was in no way about manners; it was about survival. A single wrong word, a perceived defiance, could escalate with terrifying speed—morphing from a stern look to a public humiliation, or worse, an act of violence. A desecration of another Black body. These were the invisible shackles, tighter than any chain, that held us bound. For they bound not just our limbs but our aspirations.

While I was fortunate not to experience these things directly, I was not shielded from the conversations that went on about these happenings in other parts of the country. But moths do not remain moths forever, and only in leaving their cocoons do they ever become butterflies. That was the beginning of the unraveling for me. I was beginning to grow, to see that the world was beautiful—but it was also dangerous out there.

OUR PEOPLE

They were ancient, those elders—or so they seemed to my eight-year-old eyes. They often felt like gods, though now I know they were only forty, sometimes fifty, years beyond my own tender age. Yet in their presence, time itself seemed to bend, folding in on itself to reveal the deep, gnarled roots of our lineage.

Family values were not a political statement used to deny rights like abortion; they were the very bedrock upon which our lives were built. We were taught, with a seriousness that bordered on survival and preservation, that these older folks were not just kin but living libraries—repositories of wisdom gleaned from fields of hardship and harvests of joy. You'd be surprised, truly, at the quiet profundity that could be drawn from their knowing silences, their steady gazes, and the rhythm of their hands as they shelled peas or mended clothes.

I was sixteen when we moved from Appleton Street to Dolfield Street in 1961, about a seventeen-minute drive away. Dolfield was different from Appleton. It's interesting how a place can just... sink into your bones. I guess it's because this was the place where my life changed. Forever.

When I revisit the old neighborhood these days, it looks quite a bit smaller than I remember. I guess a child's eye sees everything as bigger. Unlike Appleton, Dolfield was a larger community, with little detached houses and rowhomes dotting both sides of the long street. It started at the traffic light on Hilton Street and ended at Garrison Boulevard, with several streets branching off it. Our little detached bungalow sat between Ridgewood Avenue and Oakford Avenue.

Dad had been holding onto some money from his GI Bill benefits. The GI Bill—or the Servicemen's Readjustment Act, as they called it officially—was supposed to help all the fellas who'd fought in the Second War get back on their feet. It was for things like going to college, getting job training, or even buying a house with a low-interest loan. For white veterans, it was like a golden ticket to a whole new life—they could buy homes in the new suburbs, go to big universities, and build up a real future.

But for most Black veterans, it was different. Daddy didn't talk about it much, but Mama would sometimes mention how many colored boys who fought overseas came home and couldn't get a dime of those benefits. Banks wouldn't give them loans for houses, even with the GI Bill guarantee. Colleges either wouldn't let them in or steered them to small vocational schools instead of real universities. And out in the suburbs, there were whole neighborhoods—brand new and shiny—that had rules against Black families buying homes there.

It was like they wanted our men to fight and die for the country, but not to actually live in it. Daddy was one of the lucky few. He'd saved his money and, after years of looking, found a house in a newer development on Dolfield, a place where colored folks were starting to move in.

Our homes—the Black House—were many things. Shelters from the biting wind and scorching sun of the outside world, yes, but more than that, they were crucibles of morality, laboratories where character was forged. We were taught to listen—truly listen—like our lives depended on it. And they did. Discipline was a constant companion, that unseen hand guiding us away from the precipice of foolishness. Respect actually meant something—a sacred offering to those who had paved the way and seen the sun before you, even by a minute.

There was no tolerance for foolishness, no quarter given to ill manners. If something wasn't right, if a word was spoken out of turn, or if a gesture betrayed disrespect, they weren't having it. The consequence wasn't always a switch or a belt; most times it was that all-too-familiar chilling weight of a disappointed gaze, a silence that was more painful than the belt.

And yet, within this strict architecture of righteousness, there was always—always—the chance to talk. The tongue was never bound in our household. Questions, doubts, and even fledgling arguments were permitted, sometimes even encouraged, so long as they were offered with the requisite deference. Talking was never an issue. It was the breath of our shared life, the means by which understanding bloomed.

And we talked—loudly. The men around the corner

stores, the women around the kitchen table and on the front porch, and the kids—we ran everywhere, and every Black house was our house.

I can say, with a clarity born of hard-won wisdom from the years, that we stopped raising our children and allowed the system that never understood them in the first place to raise them. You are the parent, and it's your responsibility. Unless there's something truly detrimental that's happened to the family—some profound rupture—they're not anyone else's responsibility. The community is here to guide and to help, to offer the wisdom of those ancient elders, but not to take over the sacred charge that belongs to the parents, just as our own parents didn't pass it off to anyone else.

There is a certain power in community that the American brand of capitalism shuns. And rightly so. Because community means sharing, and sharing, they say, is caring.

My mother, barely more than a child herself, had me at seventeen. With my biological father off fighting in the war, she was saddled with the responsibility of single motherhood. But she was fortunate to have my grandparents. And on days when she had to go take care of her clients, a different kind of sanctuary awaited me. I spent the afternoons with the Taylors, a West Indian couple. I can still smell the lingering aroma of spices and herbs that filled the air of their kitchen.

This existence—this freedom to simply be a child and be seen as a child—taught me the meaning of community.

Shared meals. Shared stories. Shared humanity. My grandparents raised me, happily, until Mama met John Singleton—Daddy—and they got married.

Daddy worked at Bethlehem Steel—at one time the largest steel company and credited with much of New York's skyline—for thirty-five years until he was laid off. I saw Daddy as a man of steel himself, not just in his labor but in his bearing. There was a quiet strength about him that seemed to defy the very laws of gravity and the crushing burdens of the world.

He was, crucially, heavily involved in the union—a brotherhood of working men, a bulwark against the raw, unvarnished exploitation that was the lifeblood of America's industrializing world. It was through him, in one of our usual conversations on the porch, that I first learned about unions and their formidable role in standing up for workers. "Sweet Popper the Grasshopper," or "Big John," as he was popularly called by his peers, led not only at home but in the community too. Together with the other men in the neighborhood, he formed the Dolfield Athletic Association—one of several Little League and "Pony" League baseball teams established to keep the young boys engaged and out of trouble.

The sun had melted itself into a generous dollop of butter on toast, warming the weathered planks of the porch. I sat on the upper steps with my knees crouched between my elbows, watching a robin tug at something from the ground

—a worm, maybe. Daddy was settled into his creaking chair with the day's sweat still clinging to his work shirt like a second skin as he flipped through the pages of *The Baltimore Afro-American.*

Membership in the labor unions had peaked, and corporations had already begun opposing compulsory unionism. Individual sentiments toward "the right-to-work" had started creeping in slowly. Talk about unions was everywhere. To my child's mind, I couldn't quite understand what it was all about.

"Daddy," I chirped, turning toward him, "Why's everyone talking about a union meeting? What's a union? "

His gaze, usually fixed on the far horizon of his thoughts, turned to me, his eyes crinkling at the corners.

"Well now, Janet-girl, that's a good question. A union, you see, is like a family—but for folks who work the same kind of job. Like the men at the factory or the women down at the textile mill."

He leaned forward, his voice softening to a low rumble, like distant thunder promising rain.

"Back in the day, before unions, a man could work himself to the bone, from sunup to sundown, and still barely keep a roof over his head. The bosses—they held all the cards, Janet. They could say, 'You work for this little, or you don't work at all.' And a man with mouths to feed had little choice but to bow his head."

He paused, a shadow passing over his face like a cloud.

"But then some brave souls, they started to talk to each other. How about we all stood together? ' they said. 'What if we spoke with one voice instead of a hundred small ones? And that's what a union is, Janet. It's that one voice. It's folks gathering up their courage, like picking wildflowers in a field, and saying, 'We deserve better. We deserve fair pay for fair work. We deserve a safe place to earn our bread.'"

I chewed on my lip, picturing men holding hands, forming a giant circle against a looming factory.

"So, they make the bosses listen? " I asked.

"Exactly, darlin'." He nodded in a slow, deliberate movement. "They bargain, you see. They say, 'We'll work hard, we'll make your goods, but in return, you have to treat us right. You have to give us wages that can feed our children and keep them warm. You have to make sure the machines don't swallow up our fingers, or the dust don't choke our lungs.' And when enough folks stand together, the bosses—they have to listen. Because without the workers, Janet-girl, there ain't no factory."

He stretched his legs, his work boots thudding softly on the porch.

"It isn't always easy, mind you. There have been hard fights and real struggles. Folks have gone without pay and faced down threats—all to make sure the next generation, your generation, has a better chance. It's about dignity, Janet. It's about knowing your worth and not letting anyone tell you otherwise. It's about the right to earn a living wage and come home safe to your family at the end of the day."

The robin, satisfied with its catch, flew off with a triumphant flap of its wings. It was about dignity—about drawing a line in the unforgiving dirt and declaring, "This *far, and no further."* These were not abstract concepts; they were the very sinews of our survival, a shield against the ceaseless, grinding force of the American lie.

And Daddy? This was the Black man—in his home, in his community—standing tall, providing, protecting. The anchor. Holding down his own in the treacherous currents of a society built on his subjugation, yet still managing to bring home the bacon and to instill a sense of order and purpose. This was a man whose very existence was evidence of defiance, a living rebuke to the centuries-long project of the American state to diminish, to emasculate, to render him invisible or, worse, criminal.

From the auction block, where his body was reduced to chattel and his family torn to the sharecropper's field, where debt was a new form of bondage, to the brutal, dehumanizing era of Jim Crow, where his very manhood was under constant assault—the system had always sought to dismantle the Black man's place. And it appears it has succeeded.

Now, in the industrial belly of the 1950s, the battle shifted, but the war remained. He, along with the many other men of the unions, fought for a fair wage, for a safe workplace, and for the right to be seen as a man—not merely a cog in the machine, not merely a threat.

Daddy had some strict rules, which seemed to hang invisibly around the walls of our home. When it came to academics or intellectual pursuits, I was given free rein—encouraged to devour books, to question, to explore the boundless landscapes of knowledge. But when it came to parties, the world of adolescent frivolity, there was an unyielding decree: I had to take my younger brother Wesley with me. A feeble attempt, perhaps, to shield me from the unseen dangers of the world.

People would often ask Wesley, with a bemused chuckle, why he never introduced them to me. He'd feign exasperation, shrug theatrically, and say, "What do you need an introduction for? " Then, with a conspiratorial wink, he'd follow it up with, "That's because she's always buried in her books. There's no way I was going to introduce you to her!" It was a lighthearted jab, but it spoke volumes about the different paths we were encouraged to walk and the different expectations placed upon us, all under the watchful, protective eye of our father.

And while our home, like many in our community, was a bastion of order and love, it would be a lie—a dangerous romanticizing—to say there were no instances of abuse among families at the time. The pressures were immense, the wounds deep, and sometimes the strain would manifest in ways that brought pain. But it wasn't as rampant or common as it is today, a truth that speaks to the unraveling that would come later, as the forces of oppression found new, more insidious ways to dismantle the Black family—and particularly, to further diminish the Black man's presence.

Dolfied became a canvas, and my brother Wesley and I became the artists. Every corner, every laughter-filled afternoon, became brushstrokes painting the memories that would define our lives. Some people are born with a light, and Wes was one of them. He had this rare ability to make everyone feel like they mattered—not out of politeness, but because he genuinely cared. When he looked at you, he didn't just glance—he *saw* you.

Even in our tight little bungalow, with pennies stretched and spaces cramped, he filled the air with his easy laughter. Our childhood was equal parts chaos and fierce loyalty. I remember us whispering secrets late into the night, his curiosity pulling questions out of the dark. He wanted to know everything—about school, about the world beyond Dolfield, and about the *why* of things. I'd try to play the older, wiser sister, but more often than not, his earnest questions stopped me cold. Wes had this way of slicing through all the noise and getting right to the heart of it—without even trying. And sometimes, I realized he was teaching me.

He taught me patience. He taught me how to notice joy in the smallest of things. And even later in life, when the cruelest kind of shadow fell across him, that light never dimmed. When the diagnosis came—pancreatic cancer, heavy as a death knell—he didn't retreat. Instead, he opened himself up even more. Not for pity, but for connection. He shared his story so others might feel less alone in theirs. He bore that unbearable burden with a grace that still humbles me.

One time, years later, I was at a crab restaurant, picking through a pile of steaming shells, when a man came up to me. "You must be Janet!" he said, his whole face lighting up with recognition. I froze for a second, a little wary, then nodded. "Yeah, that's me."

He explained that he had just been talking with my brother Wesley. Wes had shared his story—his fight, his faith, his life—and it had clearly left its mark. The man's eyes shone with admiration. "He's amazing," he said. "I'll pray for him every day." I smiled, warmth spilling through me, and simply answered, "I know. He loves his sister."

That was Wesley. He didn't just make friends—he made family everywhere he went. His love spilled beyond bloodlines, beyond our block. Neighbors, acquaintances, and even strangers all seemed to feel it. He carried a warmth that turned connection into belonging.

Dolfield was also where I began to push against Daddy's rules. I was seventeen then, testing what it meant to be a "real" teenager. One time I decided to throw a party at the house. Daddy had a secret stash tucked away in the basement—tiny bottles of liquor, hidden for special occasions or maybe for his own quiet evenings after the mill. I pretended not to know about them, but Gary and his boys? They had a nose for mischief. Before long, a few of those bottles sat empty, their secret already gone.

Daddy found out—of course he did. His face wasn't angry, not exactly, but it was set like stone. Disappointed. That was worse than anger. "One party on Dolfield," he muttered, shaking his head. "And that's all you get." He didn't need to raise his voice; the words cut clean and final. That was the last party I ever held in our house. My newfound freedom shrank a little after that, but deep down I knew it was only the beginning. If I couldn't break loose inside, I'd find a way outside those front doors.

And trouble? Lord, we found it often. The kind that made Mama's face clench like a fist. When I did get punished, it carved itself deep into me; I learned quickly not to repeat the same mistake. Mama was good—unyielding good, the kind that feels like standing before a mountain. But punishing me? That wasn't her way. She'd sigh, weary and sharp, and say, "I don't want to punish her; it just makes me angry," as if my mistakes weren't just childish antics but betrayals of the quiet pact we shared.

Still, the worst punishment of all came disguised in play, wrapped in the shimmering innocence of childhood mischief. We'd just gotten one of those new 10-speed bikes for Christmas. Granddaddy, in the middle of remodeling the house on Appleton Street, had stripped the floors bare. And I, with my devil's spark, convinced Wesley—always curious, always easy to sway—to play "messenger service." I hooked a can of lime-green paint to his bike, and we raced through the empty rooms, our laughter bouncing off the walls.

Then it happened. Wesley hit a piece of wood, the bike jolted, and the can exploded. Lime-green everywhere. Across the walls, dripping down windows, splattered across Granddaddy's freshly sanded floors. The sound of our laughter died quickly, replaced by the silence of doom. That house, once echoing with our play, now looked like the scene of a crime.

We tried to clean it—Lord, did we try. Wads of newspaper in our little hands, frantic and futile, only smeared the bright catastrophe deeper into the floorboards, spreading the disaster like a wound. My mother, who worked at the school for delinquent girls, had seen every shade of human error. And still, knowing she would soon step into this, I was a nervous wreck all day.

When she walked in, her eyes widened, tracing the lime-green destruction that sprawled across walls and floor. Punishment was swift—both Wesley and I bore it—but it wasn't her vengeance that stung; it was her wisdom. Later, when she had cooled, she reminded us in that steady, deliberate voice, "You're *a child, and you'll do things because you don't know better. But if the same mule kicks you twice, it's your fault.*" Those words cut cleaner than any switch.

Grandfather, with his quiet strength, came to the rescue.

He didn't scold or sigh; he just got down on his knees and began scrubbing, steady and methodical, like he was erasing our folly stroke by stroke. His patience washed away more than paint; it softened the shame and turned the punishment into a lesson, one that never left me. After that, the itch for such wild, mischievous games evaporated like smoke in the wind.

Not long after, Daddy ripped out the old coal bin and poured concrete, converting the basement from a dark, dusty maw into something new—a playroom, a sanctuary for me, Wesley, and Irvin. Down there, in that cool, dim space, I became "Miss Teacher." I'd line up imaginary students, pull Wesley into my lessons when his boy-energy got too loud, and mimic the authority I had seen in my real classrooms. My voice would rise in its best imitation of discipline, echoing off the concrete walls. From upstairs, Mama would call down, her tone a mixture of exasperation and fondness: *"Miss Teacher!"* she'd say, and in that single phrase was recognition—that even in play, the seeds of my future self were already sprouting.

By the time I hit junior high, I was well into knowing what was perceived as "good" or "right" in my house. Maybe not necessarily *good* in some grand moral sense, but definitely *right*—the way things were supposed to be done according to Mama and Daddy. It was the rhythm of our lives, the unspoken rules that guided everything from how you greeted elders to how you saved every single penny. It was about respect, about working hard, about keeping your head down and not drawing undue attention to yourself—especially once we moved to the new house.

It meant doing your homework without being asked, speaking politely, dressing modestly, and always, always being home before dark. It meant going to church every Sunday, even if you sometimes caught yourself dozing off during the sermon. It meant not talking back, not questioning too much, and certainly not bringing any kind of trouble to the front door.

Above all, we talked to each other. And I don't mean over small screens glued to our fingers. Real talk. If I saw you, I'd talk to you. We had no other way to pass the time or get our news. It wasn't like today, with a TV in every room buzzing all the time. Our first television came much later, bought by my grandmother. She said it was a window to the world. But even then, watching TV was a special occasion. For me, it was mostly weekends—the Westerns on Saturday mornings and Ed Sullivan on Sunday evenings. Shows like *It's Over* were the kind of good, wholesome programs she approved of.

During the week, though, that screen stayed dark. There was no argument, no begging. It was just understood. The moment I walked through the door after school, Mama or Daddy would be right there with, "Where's the book? I know you've got homework." There wasn't even a question like, "Do you have homework?" None of that. It was assumed. If you were in school, you had something to do when you came home in the evening—and it involved books, not blinking lights.

And when we weren't doing homework or house chores, we were hanging out with the other kids in the neighborhood. The ones I was given—and given them early—were cleaning the bathroom and scrubbing the kitchen floor. Mama was the cook, and she handled the kitchen's daily cleaning, but once she was done, that floor was mine. I'd get down on my hands and knees with a bucket of soapy water, scrubbing until it shined, or until Mama declared it "right."

Wesley, on the other hand, had the outside steps. He was younger, so I guess they figured it was a boy's job—or maybe just less precise than the inside work. Sometimes he'd mess them up, leaving streaks or missing a spot, and Mama would sigh, looking at me. "Janet," she'd say, her voice low but firm, "your brother made a mess of those steps outside." And usually, that meant I'd end up out there, redoing his work.

Wes always did his own thing, our Wesley. At nineteen, he told Daddy he was leaving Dolfield and wouldn't be back. And that's exactly what he did. He enlisted in the Navy and left our Baltimore streets to serve during the Vietnam War. When he came back, he was honorably discharged in the summer of 1972. That September, he joined General Motors, where he worked for the next twenty-eight years.

He lived with his girlfriend Faith for a while, then married her. Later, they divorced. After that, he lived with another girlfriend. There wasn't a lot of back-and-forth with Wes—no second-guessing, no meandering. He just did his thing, always following his own compass, no matter where it led him. He truly was a force of nature, our Wesley. My Wes.

But you know, Mama always found a way to help me escape any hard feelings. She understood that sometimes, after the lessons and the scoldings, a girl needed something more—something to nurture the spirit. She knew I needed a path to bloom outside of just the house and the church. So she put me in charm school, where I learned poise and grace. She enrolled me in modern dance classes, where I could move and express myself in ways words couldn't capture. And she even had me in a prospective Zeta class, one of the Divine Nine groups, opening my eyes to a world of sisterhood and service that felt so grown-up and exciting.

Daddy, on the other hand, kept me firmly rooted in the church. Sundays weren't optional; they were the cornerstone of our week. And it wasn't just about sitting in the pews either. I was always volunteering—teaching Sunday school to the littlest ones, spending long, hot summers at vacation Bible school. Our lives, especially back then, revolved around what was close by. Everything was within walking distance. You walked to church, you walked to school, and you walked to the store. Our world was contained, but within those familiar streets of Baltimore, Mama and Daddy each carved out their own ways of shaping us—giving us different kinds of wings to try and fly. These were the blessings of family.

But we never escaped the curse of it. That long, winding river full of memory, streaming down bloodlines and forming arteries in each generation. It is easy to say, "I will do better than my parents did." But most times, becoming better parents eludes you, while the pressures of survival override everything else.

2

THE ROAD WE TROD

The air in Baltimore, even in those fragile, fleeting moments of childhood, carried a different kind of current in the year of my ninth birthday. It was 1954, and the city, like a vast breathing creature, was exhaling the lingering dust of an old order even as the fierce winds of change began to stir. I was a small girl with eyes that saw more than they understood, moving through streets that were both playground and battleground. The Civil Rights Movement had begun with a quiet tremor that could be felt in the taut silences of the grown-ups. The threads were pulling loose. The bombings in Birmingham had already stolen four Black girls at a Baptist church. Medgar Evers was already dead. The U.S. government—that long white house on a hill—had been slow and cautious in its concern, issuing proclamations while the South bled. We learned about lynchings not from books, but from blood—our own family trees. Like Daddy's brother, who was lynched in Columbia, South Carolina. They said he whistled at a white woman. That's all it took. That was twenty years before I ever drew breath. And yet, it haunted me. It warned the Black boys around me.

The church. The Black church was where I began to understand what the Civil Rights Movement was all about. The activism was just as loud as the praise and worship—a fortress of faith and a furnace where the spirit of our people was forged. Strategies were whispered in corners, courage preached from the pulpit, and hope for a better future nurtured. It was in those brown, holy pews that we were reminded of our inherent dignity, our God-given right to stand tall, even when the world outside tried to push us down.

The hymns—sung with voices full of yearning and defiance—were the soundtrack of this new fight. The church leaders, men and women of immense moral authority, carried dual roles: messengers of God and messengers of the various civil rights leaders and movements spreading across the country. The church was where protests were planned, where activists organized, and where weary people found the strength to keep going when the road grew too hard.

The sermons then hit differently. We were Black Israelites, and God was leading us into battle—a fight not just for our rights, but for our very lives. The pews felt charged with a different kind of energy on Sunday mornings when the preacher spoke of Moses leading the Israelites out of Egypt. "One day," he'd say, "God will deliver us from this bondage too. Change is coming. Just you wait and see."

And indeed, change was coming. The movement had already spilled beyond the four corners of the colored churches and into the streets and courtrooms. That was the year of *Brown v. Board of Education,* the decision that split the country's skin open. The Supreme Court handed down a ruling meant to end segregation in public schools, but the country itself had no intention of healing—or at least it was not ready.

Desegregation, they called it. As though a single word could undo centuries of deprivation. As though a pen in Washington could convince Mississippi to lay down its rage or transform the sneer on a white child's face into a smile. We knew better. It was natural knowledge: white folks didn't want us in their schools.

In our segregated Black schools, we had smart Black teachers and administrators who knew what was coming. We were just kids—we didn't yet understand the weight of the responsibility ahead of us. But our teachers knew this war demanded preparation, and that is exactly what they gave us. The Eisenhower administration may have parted the Red Sea, but it was the Black leaders in our community—our churches, our book clubs, the NAACP, and the Urban League—who led us through.

These were the years of total liberation. Every Black man, woman, and child was a soldier. We read about our history and learned about the people who paved the way. We weren't just being taught history—we were making it. We sang songs about Harriet Tubman and Sojourner Truth as if they were cousins, not distant legends. Ours has always been a fight that requires memory—a remembering and a *reminding*—to armor us. Sweet armor in the form of stories, hymns, and truths that had never been printed in our textbooks.

Because they knew. Our teachers, our mothers, our uncles in the NAACP, the gallant warriors in the Urban League—they all knew. They knew we were being sent into a battlefield disguised as a school hallway. That we would face spit and slurs. That the government had opened the doors, but not the hearts of the people behind them. This land we built did not want us in it. But as Baldwin said, "the place in which I'll fit will not exist until I make it."

And so the fight began. Lord, weren't we making it? Crafting belonging out of nothing. Building dignity out of dust. We were the generation to begin the harvest—the fruits of the labor of our heroes past.

Even the selection, I came to understand, was meticulous. Handpicked like grade-A cherries bound for Buckingham. Of course, it had to be on their terms. *Model Black kids.* Good grades, calm, not defiant, from "good homes," adaptable. The ones who could endure relentless scrutiny and chilling indifference. The bullying.

Garrison Junior High, a public school in a predominantly Jewish area of Baltimore County, was a world away—not in miles, but in the rift of expectation and perceived difference. It was a place where my skin would be the loudest thing about me, constantly announcing itself in rooms where every other face was pale. After years of being among my own and seeing myself as the rule, I was suddenly thrown into the reality that I was, in fact, the exception. The minority.

I was one of fourteen. Fourteen Black children, like pearls tossed into the sea, expected to swim with no help, no mercy. They had their systems—separate schedules, staggered lunch times, different teachers, the same textbooks but different questions. Fourteen girls. Yet never in the same class. We were scattered across schedules to ensure no two Black students ever sat in the same room.

Still, we did not break.

The belonging was always going to be a mirage, a cruel trick of the light. Stepping into that classroom on the first day of school—suddenly, sharply—among all those white children, was a kind of desecration. It was a violent psychological wrenching, even if no hand was raised and no cruel word was spoken aloud in my hearing. It was the sudden, shattering awareness that the very ground of my being—my Blackness, my history, my family, the comforting loudness of my community—was seen as *other*. Not just different, but lesser. Something to be endured, perhaps, but never embraced.

This desecration—this violation—wasn't in a punch or a shove. It was in the cold, curious stares. The averted eyes. The way their laughter seemed to stop just short of including me. It was in the sudden, sharp silence that fell when I entered a group, the unspoken reminder that I was outside, beyond the circle of their easy camaraderie. It was the constant, low-grade tap of being a spectacle, a symbol, rather than simply a child named Janet.

It does something to you, you know. This constant vigilance, this hyper-awareness of your own skin in a room full of theirs. It was a cruel lesson: that the color of my skin was always a question mark in their eyes. A problem to be solved—or, more often, ignored. An assault on my soul, on our souls, on the souls of Black folk.

My mother made sure my gym uniform was starched and ironed every week. She wanted me to look just right so they couldn't find one more reason to criticize me. And rightly so—because our elders had already been through so much, and they did everything they could to keep us from absorbing all that nastiness.

One day, while in class—and I did not recall this memory until a former classmate reminded me recently—the teacher asked a question, then turned toward the room and said,

"Who wants to answer? Can I see those little creamy white hands up?"

I don't know where the rebellious spirit came from, but I pumped my fist into the air. The whole classroom went quiet. After a few seconds of awkward stares, she chose a white girl to answer her question.

But the fight was only beginning. Black folk didn't just want the right to a fair education; they wanted the promise America extended to others to be theirs as well. Momentum was building, and the civil rights leaders were becoming more vocal and more difficult to ignore. The *Brown v. Board of Education* decision had opened a floodgate. If we could share the same classrooms, then perhaps we could also share water fountains and public buses equally.

It was in this same year, 1954, that I joined my first protest. It wasn't rage that led me—not yet—it was readiness. Because at that point, I did not yet know what it meant to feel anger toward America's dehumanization of Black folk. We had a book club led by the wife of a Black doctor—a woman who never raised her voice but carried thunder in her eyes. We read Baldwin and Du Bois before we could fully understand them. We read for survival. For clarity. For language we could wield when facing white librarians who wouldn't let us borrow books, or white girls who rolled their eyes when we answered questions in class. And when I got to Morgan State, I met more women like her. Women like the wife of Rev. Cornish. He was the chaplain, but it was his wife who moved the earth. She gathered us like Moses's mother gathering the baby in the reeds, and she preached to us the truth of our strength. She taught us where to stand at the sit-ins and how to sit still when they pushed us, spat at us, and called us everything but our names.

There was a kind of wisdom that carried the wings of the Civil Rights Movement. This wisdom was careful, deliberate, organized, and strategic. And for good reason. We could not falter. For the slightest mistake, America was waiting—club in hand—to justify the destruction of yet another Black body. Armed with this knowledge, we planned every move, calculated every step, and moved with the stealth of a panther.

The following year, on December 1, 1955, we heard that a Black woman, Rosa Parks, had refused to give up her seat on a bus down in Montgomery, Alabama. How dare she! The country was beginning to unravel. Before long, we were staging plays of her heroic act at church. But Rosa Parks was just one of many women in this fight for our lives. Memory is a fragile, slippery thing. It weaves in and out like smoke through cracked floorboards. But Lord, I wish I could call Rosalie's face back to me—clear and whole. That name, Rosalie, is all I have left of her now. Just her name. But even a name, if you hold it long enough, can bloom like a flower in your hand.

We were paired together by the protest organizers—children with adults, elders with the young. It was no accident.

It was strategy. If one of us was taken, we needed someone to bear witness, to carry their name. The system, even back then, was a maze—cold and without sympathy. They'd snatch you up and toss you into jail without as much as a trial, and it might take days before anyone could find you, if they found you at all.

Rosalie was older, and I was the young one. So if the police came—and they always did—it was my job to get her ID and to memorize the shape of her name, her face, and the color of her dress. They weren't supposed to take me. I was too young. But they would take her. And we, the "footrunners," as they called us, would know exactly who was missing, who had vanished into those concrete walls. That was our job: to remember, to resist the forgetting. We did sit-ins at the lunch counter and walked in protest when needed. And when police were called, I took Rosalie's pocketbook—with her ID inside—and headed back to campus. That way, if she or the other adults were arrested; the leaders would know who was missing.

News traveled slowly for us, but when it finally arrived—whether happy or sad—we shared it along the streets like a Passover. As children, we didn't always understand the full weight of it, but we believed. These stories—legends, really, in the way they sounded to our young ears—gave us a kind of zeal. Like the day, in 1966, when word reached our little neighborhood: "A colored woman made it! In Texas! Her name's Barbara Jordan!" I was twenty-one at the time. The name rolled through the air like thunder wrapped in velvet. I didn't know who she was then, not really, but I saw the way that news lit up our community in faraway Maryland. That's how I first learned that a Black woman—dark-skinned, deep-voiced, with hair like mine—had been elected to the Texas Senate. First one since Reconstruction. First Black woman, ever.

And in 1972, not long after I left Morgan State, Barbara Jordan stood tall in the U.S. House of Representatives. It was a moment, child, a *moment.* She would later step behind a microphone during the Watergate hearings and speak not just to America, but *for* it. She spoke of the Constitution with the reverence of a woman who had been denied its promises yet claimed its power nonetheless. President Lyndon B. Johnson had seen her greatness early and pulled her close like the weapon she was. But it was her mind, her fire, and her knowing, that kept her rising.

It is not new—this pulling down of memory, this deliberate erasure. This slicing of Black history from schoolbooks, the banning of books, the fading of names that once gave us power, and the demonizing of words born from our struggle. It is intentional, this forgetting. And our children are growing up unknowing—unaware of the power they carry in their blood. They do not know what was paid, so they might sit where they sit, laugh how they laugh, vote, walk, breathe —free and unaware. These privileges were won with blood and sweat. With survival. With bent backs and shut mouths.

And yet, too many of our children do not know the names of those who bled so they could live. Careless with their freedom, fragile with their fire.

How do you stand tall if you don't even know the storm you're standing in? How can they understand what still could happen when they don't even know what already has? We remembered because we had to. We carried names like Rosalie so the world would not forget what was done. And now, I speak her name again. So you remember. So *they* remember. So we don't disappear.

These recent killings of our Black boys—boys who should have been taken to jail but were shot instead, accused of some crime—show us that nothing has really changed. Same thing, just done a little differently now. But if we hadn't known our history, I don't think we could have done what we did. We had to understand what had already changed because of that history. It helped dispel some of our fears, as scared as we were. Because the question was always there: *What could happen?* Would they take you to the woods and lynch you, like they'd always done?

Desegregation — My year group at Garrison Junior High School, Baltimore (1956)

3
BEFORE COURAGE HAD A NAME

It was the summer of 1962, a year after we moved from Appleton to Dolfield Avenue. I had just turned seventeen, preparing for my final year of high school at Eastern. I carried my own dreams for the future: to get an education, secure a good job, build a career, start a family, and see the world beyond Baltimore. I had always wanted to be a social worker—an ambition, perhaps, born from years of watching the women before me tend to others with such care. I wanted to take care of people, too.

Seventeen is a strange and sacred age. It's the edge of the river, where a girl can still see her reflection clearly before stepping into waters that run deeper than she can understand. I was seventeen when I first felt the press of romance, the stirrings of a heart that didn't yet know itself. Seventeen makes you bold and naïve, makes you believe love is everything and forever. It fills your chest with foolish fire and fantasy. But it carries no map, no compass—only dreams and a beating heart.

Daddy was very strict when it came to me interacting with boys. "You're still very young. Focus on your books," he would say.

I made a new friend when we moved to Dolfield—Cynthia. She lived with her parents just down the street on Columbus Drive. We both attended Eastern High, though she was two years behind me. Cynthia's house became our gathering place most evenings, where the girls—and sometimes the boys from the neighborhood—would sit around talking.

It was on one of those evenings, in the summer of '62, that I met Leroy. He wasn't from our block, but he visited his parents, who lived just behind us on Callaway Avenue. We were all hanging out on Aunt Molly's porch when he first spoke to me. Boys spoke to me all the time, but this felt different. His tone was different. And there, in that quiet moment, I felt the peculiar, exquisite tremor of being seen—not as Janet the dutiful daughter or Janet the diligent student—but as something more. Interesting.

Everything felt heightened then, almost unbearable in its intensity. We spent long hours talking and laughing. He would tell me everything about himself—or at least, that's what I thought. Gradually, I became comfortable in his company. More than comfortable—I began to look forward to it, to anticipate the evenings when I would see him again.

Our relationship didn't really take shape until 1963. At first, we were just getting to know each other. He was the first boy I ever really talked to like that, the first I spent time with. We weren't going on dates—it was porch talks, summer strolls, and neighborly visits. By then, I had graduated from Eastern High and was starting at Morgan State, and that's when we began seeing each other more regularly.

Looking back now, from the vantage point of eighty years lived and the slouched wisdom that only time can bestow, I wouldn't call it love—not the real kind, not with him. Maybe it felt close because he was the first. The first tremor in the earth. The first crack in the rigid shell of my girlhood, revealing a vulnerability I hadn't known I possessed. The intensity of that feeling, the sheer newness of it, could easily have been mistaken for the deep, abiding force that true love becomes. But it lacked the bedrock of understanding, the quiet patience, and the profound recognition of another's soul that I would later come to know.

It was more about the reflection of myself I saw in his eyes—the giddy thrill of being chosen, of being the object of such concentrated attention. And at the time, that was enough. All that mattered was that I enjoyed his company.

He had a sister, a twin—I don't remember her name—

and a brother called Michael. Every summer he'd come visit the family on Callaway. So, when he returned in the summer of '63, my body was already reeling from the missed moments of the year before. Yearning for him. I had just turned eighteen and felt the thrill of adolescence tingling in me. The world narrowed to the space between us, yet at the same time expanded into an infinite field of sensation. My skin felt new, alive, and hyper-aware of his nearness. Every word he spoke, every flicker of his eyes, became a puzzle I longed to solve.

It was a vulnerability I hadn't known before—a handing over of a part of myself I didn't even realize existed into the unsteady hands of another. Another I would later come to know I didn't really know. But at the time, there was a thrill in it. A thrill born of daring, of breaking from the unspoken rules that governed a young Black woman's body in that era. It was the quiet defiance of claiming my own desires, of acknowledging a self that had long been hidden, even from me.

There was a raw, physical awakening—foreign yet intimate. The mixing of breath, of skin, of unspoken promises in the dark. But beyond the physical was the deeper thrill of the secret itself, the knowledge that I had stepped into a new realm, one that set me apart from the girls who still only dreamt. It felt like initiation, a private rite of passage into the fullness of being—where my body, my desires, and my womanhood began to speak a language all their own.

And it was in one of those moments that the seed was planted—the seed that would change the trajectory of my life and, dare I say, the world.

The first signs came like whispers of doom. A sudden wave of nausea, the foods I once craved now making my stomach churn. A missed cycle that stretched into weeks of gnawing anxiety. And then, the truth solidified—a hard, undeniable knot in my belly. I was pregnant. But for an eighteen-year-old girl in 1963, it was not the sweet anticipation of motherhood I felt. It was suffocating terror. Pregnancy at my age could mean the end of every dream, every carefully laid plan for a future beyond Dolfield's weary streets. And yet even that fear didn't prepare me for what came next.

His mother was shocked when Daddy and I went to their house, breaking the news that I was pregnant and Leroy was the father. A week later, she and her husband returned with the verdict—there was nothing they could do. Leroy already belonged to another life. He lived with a woman, and together they had three children.

The revelation struck like scalding water poured over bare skin. Betrayal. Erasure. Everything I thought we had was exposed as nothing more than illusion. The shame came quickly, heavy and relentless—the shame of my naiveté, of believing in something that never truly existed. How could I have known? That a twenty-two-year-old man, who had looked into my eyes and pulled me into his orbit, already had a household of his own. That I had surrendered such an intimate, uncharted part of myself to someone whose world was already full.

As days became weeks and weeks stretched into months, the world—which had imploded with the revelation of Leroy's tangled life—settled into a terrifying stillness. It was the quiet after the earthquake, when the dust hung heavy and the true devastation slowly revealed itself. I was pregnant. This soft, undeniable life growing inside me was no longer a secret; it was a future—monstrous in its unknown shape—demanding to be reckoned with. The dizzying thrill of first intimacy had soured into a bitter understanding: connection can deceive, and vulnerability is a dangerous gift.

Daddy, whose sternness was as much a part of our home as the brick it was built from, had already delivered his verdict. "Any decision you make now is for the two of you— you and that baby." His words struck like iron, stripping me of the last vestiges of reckless youth. In that moment, he felt like the meanest man in the world, laying the weight of permanence on my still-girlish shoulders.

The days that followed were a long siege within myself. My body was no longer fully my own. My mind was a battlefield. Daddy, in his stark pragmatism, had narrowed the path before me. Dr. Hall, our family doctor, whose voice usually carried the balm of reassurance, confirmed what I already feared: I was too far along. Too far for abortion even to be an option. That door had shut. The choices that remained were few and unforgiving: give birth and place the child for adoption, or leave school and become a mother.

But my mother and grandmother—those two women who knew the deepest contours of my heart—understood what no man, however well-meaning, could. Mama's words, soft but steady, became my anchor: "Don't let John push you into making a decision. The decision is yours, but just know we are behind you."

The options before me felt like two sharp stones in my hand, each promising a different kind of pain, a different exile from the girl I had been. And whichever I chose would shape not only my life but also another's. For nine months, I carried two pregnancies: the quiet life growing in my womb and the one in my head—a relentless storm of questions, fears, and imagined futures. That second pregnancy, the unseen one, was perhaps the more brutal. It was the constant, agonizing battle between two fates: the stark pragmatism of putting the child up for adoption, a path that promised a return to the future I had once imagined, or the terrifying leap into motherhood, a commitment that, to my eighteen-year-old self, felt like stepping into an uncharted wilderness. I walked Baltimore's streets with a belly full of questions and a heart strung tight between two destinies. And always, Daddy's words—"Any decision you make now is for two of you"—hung over me like storm clouds refusing to move.

He was born on a Friday, February 28, 1964. A raw, primal tearing that left me exhausted, emptied, and trembling with both pain and awe. I heard his cry the moment they pulled him from me—a small, indignant wail that pierced the sterile air and lodged itself deep inside my soul. But I did not see him. I did not touch him. They didn't let me. Not until Sunday afternoon—two days later, two days of the world holding its breath, two days of my heart suspended between choice and consequence. Those hours were a purgatory, each minute stretching into eternity, the weight of decision pressing like a stone on my chest. And on that holy day, I chose. I chose motherhood.

When they finally brought him to me that Sunday afternoon, I braced myself. There he was: a small, squalling bundle, all soft skin and furious hunger. He looked at me—or so it felt—with ancient eyes, already knowing. And I'll say, he got me back. The very first time I offered him the bottle of Similac, he latched on with a ferocious determination, draining it down like he'd been waiting centuries. I felt a strange surge of tenderness, a recognition. And then, as if in a perfectly timed act of cosmic retribution, he turned his head and vomited it all over me. Not on the bed—on me! A warm, milky deluge covering my nightgown, my arms, and my chest.

And in that moment, a sigh—shaky, disbelieving—bubbled up from deep within me. All the fear, all the uncertainty, and all the agonizing deliberation evaporated in a sudden, messy wave of milk and baby. "Oh," I thought, a grin spreading across my face, "you're getting me back for even thinking about putting you up for adoption, huh?" The choice, which had felt so heavy, so impossible, suddenly became simple. This was my child.

He had my mother's eyes, and I gave him Daddy's surname, Singleton. For his first name, I borrowed from the heavens: John Glenn, the first man to orbit the earth, circling it three times the year before I conceived him. And so began my journey into the school of motherhood. I had dropped out of Morgan State the week before he was born. When Glenn was seven weeks old, Wesley used his connections to get me a job at a drugstore, and I went straight to work. I had been a girl, dreaming of the world, but now I was a woman with a world of my own to build. By then, it was mostly just me and Cynthia, my neighbor down the block. We stayed close, but beyond that, my life narrowed to work and the sacred, consuming responsibility of caring for my child.

I didn't see Leroy for about three years after Glenn was born, even though his parents still lived nearby. Daddy said they sometimes came by to ask how I and the baby were doing, and he'd simply tell them we were doing just fine. Then, one day in 1967, Leroy showed up. He looked at me and asked, "What do you want me to do? You want to go have a blood test done so we can go to court?"

By then, my life had already contorted itself into a new trajectory. I held no grudge against him. When I looked at his face that day, I didn't just see Leroy—I saw the whole lineage of Black men caught between the rock of their own desires and the hard place of a world that refused to let them stand. Generations of men were denied the space to fully be men, who had to fight for every breath, and in that fight had lost the language of soft things and of responsibility that wasn't forced.

My words came out clean, scrubbed of all the emotions that could have choked them. "I want to have blood work done for your certainty," I told him. "But forget about court. I don't have time for any of that." And the truth was, I didn't. Not anymore. By then, I had found something rare and fragile: a foothold in the crumbling edifice of this country. I had a new job—a good government job with the Social Security Administration, which I had started in 1965. When I looked toward the future, I saw Glenn's face in it, his small hands reaching for a world I was determined to build for him. My focus had to be on that—on him and on me.

But beneath the surface, something else was stirring—a storm I had no words for yet. Blood doesn't always mean safety, and while family is often the first place a woman learns to survive conflicting truths, sometimes a daughter must become mother to herself. That reality was dawning faster than the sun rose in the east. Frictions between Daddy and me were becoming more frequent. The bliss of being a daughter had worn off, and I was beginning to see the man through my mother's eyes. He had something to say about everything—everything. Especially about Glenn. "You let him talk back. You let him do anything. You aren't raising him right."

At first, I excused it, as daughters do. *He's just old-fashioned. He means well. He's tired.* But the truth was harder: I had spent too long seeing Daddy through the soft haze of girlhood, where every raised voice was strength and every silence was wisdom.

But grown women—women who birth, bleed, and bury pieces of themselves for their children—eventually see more clearly. The hero I once imagined was, in the end, just a man. A flawed man. And some days, I wasn't even sure if I, his own daughter, had ever truly been safe from those flaws. When his grumblings became too heavy, too dangerous to the emotional safety of my child, I made the difficult choice to leave the only nest I had ever known. After all, a butterfly must leave the cocoon if it is ever to fly. And so, when Glenn was three, I moved out.

With time, things became clearer. The side of men that every woman fears had always been there in Daddy. I was just too naïve to see it. I didn't know then what I know now. I didn't yet have the language, the wisdom, or the safety to name it. Maybe I felt it. But back then, I thought Daddy was a tall shadow of safety. That voice that could boom loud enough to hush the streets, with a hand that rested heavy on the Bible on Sundays—and heavier still on the backs of our necks when we stepped out of line. He was a provider and a protector, so we were taught to respect him. To love him. To fear him. But now I know: those things are not the same.

I remember something that happened while I was in junior high, after I developed what folks around me called "those size 66 breasts," the kind that pulled grown men's eyes like magnets and made grown women uncomfortable. My mother, maybe thinking she was helping, bought me those wide, striped tops to hide what she could. I was still a child, but my body had grown womanly overnight. I was always a little round thing, with legs too pretty to go unnoticed and feet that looked like they belonged in a pageant once I got them done. I'd wear a dress and tease a little, not knowing what danger flirted back.

That was when they stopped letting me come home after school. Wesley and I were sent to a babysitter. Not for safety from the danger that lurked in the streets, but from the one that threatened my innocence in our own home. I couldn't name it then. I just knew I was always going somewhere I didn't want to go.

The story didn't make sense then. I was old enough to catch the city bus alone, but too young to come home alone? I didn't question it. I just swallowed it, the way all little Black girls are taught to do. It wasn't until I was grown that I began to remember the pieces. Not full scenes, just flashes: cold air, someone watching, and my grandmother's sudden appearance at home one day, grabbing me and walking me two blocks away to Mama Shepard's house, like her soul had set off an alarm.

There was a kind of knowing in the women in my family —a quiet sisterhood of intuition that stretched from my grandmother's eyes to my mother's hands. Later, I would come to understand it all bordered on molestation, as they put it. Didn't "go all the way to defilement," they said, like that made it better. Like halfway harm is harm all the same. I remember my mother saying to him once, her voice trembling and low, "If you even think about it, I'll kill you."

It was finally making sense. And I believed her. Because in that moment, I saw the mother in her stand up tall. She wasn't asking. She was telling. And I think it was that same mother in me that made the decision, later on, to leave with my son.

The pedestal I had placed Daddy on crumbled fast as the years rolled by. It didn't help that he was physically violent toward my mother. Daddy had already bruised her before I even got to junior high. I had seen the marks. I recall Grandmother opening the front door and freezing in her tracks when she saw her daughter—my mother—battered and broken. I watched her walk past me as though a ghost had stepped into her bones, then knock Daddy back with a strength that didn't look like it came from this earth. She broke his glasses. Told him she'd kill him if he ever touched her daughter again.

And I believed her, too. You see, it was always the women doing the saving. Perhaps I was too young to fully understand the sickness in that house—the way power passed down through fists and yells, through cigarette lighters and locked doors, through who was allowed to rest and who was made to leave. I thought everyone got what they deserved. That was the logic of a child trying to make sense of grown-folk violence. But now, looking back, I see it clearer: Daddy deserved to get his ass kicked.

My mother was so light-skinned that her bruises glowed purple and yellow for days before fading. I can still see her face—half light, half sorrow. But she tried to live. Tried to reclaim joy, however small. On weekends, she went out with her girlfriends. Just them. Cards, drinks, laughter. No men. Just the breath of being free from him. But Daddy hated that too. He'd accuse her of sleeping with the neighborhood policeman, the one who stopped by now and then in his uniform, like he did with all the neighbors—polite and kind to the kids. Another man he couldn't control, so he made him into a threat. All the while, Daddy was messing around with our babysitter. I remember my mother confronting the girl's mother. She took me with her.

And there we were, in that kitchen—the Black woman's courtroom—where truth is served hot and cold at the same table. My mother said it plainly: "She's in a relationship with my husband." She asked about the cigarette lighter he had bought the girl. She took it back. She already knew what was going on. After that, there was no peace, only pretending.

Our family wasn't spared the drama that lived in most extended families either. The memory of my father's sisters, Aunt Florence and Aunt Bertha, hovers around like a shadow lingering at the edge of my consciousness. They didn't care for my mother—or for me. To them, we were intruders, an unwelcome presence. My mother was "one of those light-skinned Black women," lighter even than their lightest sister, the one they seemed to worship. That, I would later learn, was the root of their animosity. My mother, bless her, never explained it, and perhaps she truly didn't care.

When my father told his sisters I was pregnant, their disdain solidified. They wanted nothing to do with me. My mother brushed it off. She lived by the code that secrets were always part of Black life—secrets piled on lies. But as my father later revealed, their rejection of me was a sharp, hypocritical sting, especially considering that my cousin, three years younger, had already birthed four babies by three different men. That was the kind of intricate, messy family drama we had to navigate.

Yet in our household, my parents told it straight, and we kept moving. We were in Baltimore; they were in South Carolina. Their opinions and their judgments couldn't touch us. But knowing how they felt became a different kind of armor. I didn't step foot in South Carolina until I was fully grown—in my late thirties or early forties—for a family reunion. That was my first time there.

Even though my father married my mother in 1948, those invitations never came. Aunt Bertha, in particular, remained a distant presence until she was terminally ill in 1999. Wesley, my brother, wanted to see her before she passed, so I drove him down. It was around that time I learned she had once tried to convince my mother to give Wesley to her to raise. My mother, ever the unyielding force, had simply said no: "He's my son; he's staying with his family in Baltimore."

When Daddy first told me of his sisters' indifference—their deep-seated dislike for my mother and, by extension, for me—it wasn't a revelation. I already knew. My mother, in her blunt, honest way, had told me from the very beginning.

It was because she was a light-skinned Black woman, lighter than their cherished, lightest sister. That was the cruel irony of it: the colorism that had seeped so deep into their Southern world.

And Daddy, with his calm defiance, took immense pleasure in relaying my accomplishments, my awards, and my successes to them. It was his sharp, sarcastic way of letting them know that their opinions—their judgments—didn't matter. Not then, not ever.

With my son, Glenn

COURAGE WAS ALL SHE HAD

Teenage pregnancy hasn't always carried the shame it does now for Black folks in this country. If our history tells it true—and I believe it does—bearing children young was once a kind of power. A currency. A necessity. A Black girl's womb was property.

Our bellies fed fields, our milk nursed the sons of those who enslaved us, and our babies were either sold or sacrificed for survival. It wasn't until Black motherhood stopped profiting the world that it became a disgrace to the mother. So, when I found myself with child at eighteen, I didn't see myself as broken. I saw myself as part of a line. A continuation. Not a mistake. Still, the weight of it was unbearable some days. Not the child—Glenn was never the burden. The burden was the world's eyes on me. The burden was the whip of those glances, the way people looked at me like I had stolen my own future. But I hadn't. I had simply made a choice.

Courage was all I had when I faced that river before me—and it was courage that helped me swim across. My mother stood by me, because her knees had once buckled under that same weight. And my grandmother carried me through it because she knew too. She knew what it meant to be turned away, to be told, "Find someplace else to go." Her own father had cast her out like an unwanted seed. She never said much about it, only brushed it aside: "Forget it. Thank God I've lived this long, and I'm at peace living with you." But pain doesn't vanish—it settles into the softest parts of us and teaches us how to love better than we were loved. Somehow, she had learned to still hold some love for the man who cast her away. Once, I asked if the land Papa Williams owned was part of reparations—the forty acres and a mule. She was so offended, I never brought it up again. "No," she said, sharp as a slap. "My Pa bought that land." I hadn't meant harm; I just wanted to understand her story.

Choosing motherhood over ambition didn't mean I stopped dreaming. It meant I had to reroute the dream. I learned how to make a career in quiet spaces, in between feeding Glenn, riding the bus to work, and putting coins in the milk fund. When I first started at the Social Security Administration, I used to catch the bus each day. One afternoon, the driver sent me roses after I got off. I told my mother about it. "I don't want any roses," I said. "He should've sent a case of Pet milk for Glenn." She sat me down with a sigh so heavy it seemed to carry the weight of every woman before her. "You're going too far," she said gently. "That boy didn't have to send you anything. But he saw you. He saw you and thought you were still worth something."

That struck me. Being a single parent humbles you. Not just in spirit—but in your very flesh. It strips you down to what's essential. It teaches you that love isn't a fairy tale. It's a commitment. A series of daily, sacred acts. A choice you make again and again, especially when no one claps for it. Especially when your hands are cracked from carrying more than you should have to carry alone.

But it also teaches you joy. Not joy in the way other people hand it to you, but the kind of joy you learn to make for yourself. There is nothing small about the courage it takes to become a mother when the world gives you every reason to choose otherwise. There is nothing shameful about choosing life—not just the child's life, but your own too. I look at Glenn now, tall and good and full of purpose, changing lives around the world, and I know I did something right. And I thank the women before me who bent but didn't break, who were pushed out but never stayed gone, who taught me that ambition isn't always found sitting on a hill with a blinking beacon—it is sometimes discovered in cradles and kitchens, in rising every morning against all odds. If this life I built wasn't the one I had planned, it was certainly the one I chose. And that, more than anything else, makes it mine.

When Glenn was born and Wendell was three, my mother went back to the hospital—this time to Spring Grove. I had to have her committed. She had become overwhelmed and slipped back into crisis, though she had managed to stay out of one for ten years between Irvin's birth and Wendell's. I took Wendell in and began raising him and Glenn together. My baby brother became my son too, and I mothered him for three or four years until Mama returned home.

THE SOFTEST WARRIOR

It's amusing how society tries to romanticize redemption. But I learned early that not every story gets tied up with a bow, and not every absence deserves the dignity of closure. Some folks drift through your life like smoke through a screen door—leaving nothing but the impression of their passing and the faint scent of what might have been. That's what Leroy became for me: a lesson. Biology, I came to understand, is nothing more than cells dividing and multiplying—a scientific dance that has little to do with the sacred act of fathering. Real fatherhood lives in the daily showing up, in the steady presence that becomes a child's true north. And I learned, with a certainty that settled in my bones like morning frost, that you can love your child with every fiber of your being without spending a single moment trying to rewrite another man's failures.

The day I walked into that courthouse in 1964, the world outside was changing like seasons turning. President Johnson had just signed the Civil Rights Act that summer, and the news was filled with talk of equal rights and human dignity. But inside those cold marble halls, with their high ceilings and echoing footsteps, I discovered that some words still carried the full weight of centuries-old cruelty.

Glenn was only four or five months old then, small enough to rest in the crook of my arm, his tiny fists curled like promises against my chest. Daddy—my father, not

Glenn's—had driven me down to the courthouse with a determination that could not be bent. He was convinced we could squeeze some measure of responsibility from Leroy. "We'll get you some child support," he said, his jaw set with the kind of righteous anger that comes from watching your daughter navigate waters he couldn't calm for her. "At least get a little something for the baby."

I approached the desk, my son in my arms, my beautiful, perfect son. The woman behind the counter looked at me with eyes that had already judged and found me wanting. Her voice cut through the air like a blade when she said, "Oh, so you're here to file bastardy charges."

The word hit me like a physical blow. *Bastardy*. As if my child—this innocent baby who had done nothing but breathe, sleep, and trust the world to hold him gently—could be reduced to such ugliness. The fluorescent lights above seemed to dim, and the floor beneath my feet felt suddenly unsteady. This was 1964, and I had lived long enough to know the particular cruelty white institutions could wield, but nothing had prepared me for this moment—for hearing my child reduced to a legal term that stripped him of his humanity before he'd even had a chance to show the world his goodness.

I found myself at the public phone, hands trembling as I dialed, Glenn fussing softly in my arms as if he could sense the poison that had just been spoken over him. When Mama answered, her voice warm and familiar as Sunday morning biscuits, I broke.

"Mama," I sobbed into the receiver, tears spilling faster than I could catch them, "they called Glenn a bastard."

The silence on the other end stretched like an eternity, but I could almost hear my mother's mind working and could feel her righteous anger building like storm clouds on the horizon. When she spoke again, her voice carried the authority of generations of Black women who had learned to stand firm against a world determined to break them.

"Was that a white woman who said that to you?" Mama asked.

When I confirmed it, she continued, her words as sharp as they were steady. "She doesn't have a child—or if she does, it's still a human being. Your baby hasn't even had the chance to show them that he's a decent human being yet. Hang up that phone," she said. "Go outside, get a bus or a cab, and come home. You don't have to tolerate that. You know who your child is."

Those words wrapped around me like armor. My mother understood something fundamental about the cruelty we were up against—that some people would judge my son based on the circumstances of his birth rather than the content of his character, to borrow Dr. King's words still echoing through our collective consciousness. She knew that despite all the progress we thought we were making, there were still systems designed to shame Black women for the choices white society had often forced upon them. And Lord, how right she was.

It wasn't being a single mother that cut me to the quick—I had made my peace with that reality and had wrapped my arms around it like a coat I'd chosen to wear. What wounded me was hearing my child, my precious baby who smelled like talcum powder and possibility, reduced to something shameful in the eyes of strangers who didn't even know his name.

I walked out of that courthouse with my head held high, Glenn sleeping peacefully in my arms, oblivious to the battle that had just been fought over his worth. The bus ride home gave me time to think, to let my mother's words settle into my spirit like seeds finding fertile ground. I never went through with any of the court proceedings. Once they had reduced my child to that hateful word, there was nothing more to be said, nothing more to be negotiated.

That moment hurt me in a way I never imagined words could hurt. I had lived through the desegregation of schools and had watched grown men spit at children for the crime of wanting an education. I had heard stories of crosses burned and endured the word *"nigger"* hurled like stones. But none of that prepared me for the particular pain of hearing my innocent baby labeled with such calculated cruelty. It was different, somehow more personal, because it wasn't just about me—it was about him, about the world he would inherit, and the battles he would have to fight simply because of who his mother was.

When I got home, Mama was waiting with three-year-old Wendell on her hip, and we sat at her kitchen table while she made sense of what had happened. The late afternoon sun slanted through her yellow curtains, casting everything in golden light that made the moment feel almost sacred—two generations of Black women, trying to navigate a world determined to define us by our pain rather than our strength.

"Janet," she said, stirring sugar into her coffee with deliberate calm, "you've always read; you've always paid attention. They never should've taught you anything if they didn't want you to understand. You know the meaning and history behind these words."

And I did know. I had grown up in a community where words mattered—where the Black teachers, administrators, and parents understood the power of language to lift up or to tear down. We lived in a world where the community raised the children, where you couldn't walk down the street without some mother or father correcting you if you stepped out of line. It was a village in the truest sense, where love came with accountability and care came with consequence.

I remember those Saturday afternoons at the movies with Wesley, how by the time we made it back to the neighborhood, Mama already knew where we'd been and what time we'd gotten there. That's how tight-knit we were—a network of care and concern that wrapped around us like a safety net. Our teachers didn't need to raise their hands to correct us; a word, a look, or a raised eyebrow was enough, because we knew that message would travel faster than gossip, straight back to our parents.

In that world, I learned to pay attention to words—not just their sound, but their weight. So when that woman at the courthouse chose her weapon, I felt the full force of what she was trying to do. She was trying to shame me back into "my place," to make me accept that my child was somehow less worthy of dignity because his father had chosen absence over presence.

But I had been raised by women who understood dignity as something that comes from within, not something that can be granted or taken away by strangers behind desks. And in that moment, sitting in my mother's kitchen with the late-afternoon light painting everything gold, I made a choice that would define not just my life, but my son's understanding of his own worth.

Years later, when Glenn would stand before a room of more than a thousand people and say that I was the only person he knew who had chosen to be a parent when presented with the option not to be, I would think back to that courthouse. Back to that moment when I walked away from a system that refused to see my child's humanity. Because that's what I had done—I had chosen. Not just to give birth, but to embrace parenthood with intention and purpose, to love without apology or explanation.

The world wanted to tell me that my son was a mistake, an accident, something to be ashamed of. But I looked at his perfect little face, at his tiny fingers wrapped around mine with such trust, and I saw nothing but possibility. I saw a child who would grow up knowing that his mother had fought for his dignity before he was old enough to fight for it himself.

That day—in the middle of a decade reshaping what it meant to be Black in America—I learned that revolution sometimes looks like a mother walking out of a courthouse with her baby in her arms, choosing dignity over desperation, choosing love over legality. The Civil Rights Movement was happening in the streets and the voting booths, yes—but it was also happening in moments like these, when Black women decided their children deserved more than the scraps of respect white institutions were willing to offer.

And so I chose. I chose to be Glenn's mother in the fullest sense of the word. It was a choice I would make again and again, every day, in a thousand small ways that added up to a life of intentional love.

WILDFLOWER

Baltimore. West Baltimore. The name itself, even now, catches in my throat—a coarse melody of memory and struggle. They say wildflowers don't care where they grow, pushing up through cracks in concrete, through wood logs or hard rocks, thriving on neglect. And in a way, that's what raising a Black boy in Baltimore in the '60s and '70s felt like. It was the act of cultivating a wildflower in the harshest terrain, hoping against hope he wouldn't just survive but bloom.

It was like trying to keep a candle lit in a hurricane. You cupped your hands around the flame, prayed the wind wouldn't catch it, and hoped to God no one stomped it out before it had the chance to shine. And I cared. I cared deeply about where this wildflower of mine grew—the soil beneath his feet, the sun and rain that would nurture him. And in a city already designed to wither him, I fought to be the gardener.

The city then, in the mid-to-late 1960s, was a hotspot, the beats of the Civil Rights Movement still reverberating even as the realities of segregation and systemic oppression remained stubbornly in place. A week before Glenn celebrated his first birthday, Malcolm was assassinated in New York. Gang violence pulsed like a constant undertone. Baltimore, as the conventional wisdom went, was a place where Black boys didn't make it out. The city had a spine of steel and streets paved with concrete, both with little patience for the fragility of Black childhood.

Sandtown-Winchester. Cherry Hill. Upton. Penn-North. If you were Black and poor, your zip code wrote your whole future before you ever had a chance to dream one.

They start looking at our boys early. At five, they're "cute." At ten, they're "loud." At thirteen, they're "trouble." And by sixteen, they're suspects. This is the Baltimore Ta-Nehisi writes of in *The Beautiful Struggle*—where "to be a Black male is to be always at war." And in Baltimore, the war started young.

The city was changing, but not for us. The steel mills and factory jobs that had once offered decent pay to Black men were vanishing by the early 1970s. Unemployment was rising. Drugs began moving through the neighborhoods like a second plague—heroin first, then later crack. But even then, the wreckage was already beginning: bodies left behind, babies without fathers. Police weren't protectors; they were patrolmen. Not guardians, but guards. The schools were overcrowded and underfunded.

I can't point to a single moment and call it the worst time of my life. And that's not because life has always been easy—but because I was carried. Loved. Sheltered. Protected by hands that had already been cut on the glass of this world, yet still found the strength to wrap around me. My mothers. These women in my life made sure that whatever hurt they had seen or felt didn't land full on my shoulders. They passed me through their arms like a sacred offering—meant to be held, not harmed.

And as I grew, as I became a woman and a mother, I understood that kind of love wasn't soft—it was disciplined. It was learned. It was given. So, when I had Glenn, I knew what was required. You learn to become what once held you.

Black motherhood is part joy, part fear, and part divine preparation. It's knowing your child is sacred even when the world refuses to see it. It's holding your breath until they walk back through the door. It's loving them so fiercely that it feels like rebellion.

I was still young myself, still figuring life out. Responsibility hastened my growth. With Mother committed to a mental health institution, I took Wendell in. I was balancing so much then—Glenn was still small, barely three years younger than Wendell—and my hands were full with diapers, bus schedules, night shifts, and the parts of myself I hadn't yet untangled. I didn't have time to pause and sort through the knots in Wendell's heart. That's the hardest part about growing up in a house where everyone is doing their best: sometimes your best still isn't enough to save the ones you love.

If you asked me what shaped me most, I'd tell you: my mother. There was never any doubt about her role—she mothered her four children until the day she died. There was no off-switch in her. Her love wasn't loud or showy; it was like a familiar sound in the house you forget is playing—until it's gone.

When Glenn was four, in kindergarten, something happened that made my heart climb into my throat. It was Veterans Day, a public holiday, I think. Mr. Sims, who regularly picked him up and dropped him off, had taken him to school that morning. But it was a half-day, and he was supposed to spend the other half at Wayland Baptist Church. Only no one was there—many parents worked for the federal government and had the day off.

Mr. Sims dropped him there anyway, and when Glenn found the church empty, he set out on his own, walking from Wayland Baptist all the way to my grandmother's house in Gwynn Oak. When no one was home there either, he went next door to Connie Stokes's house—Granny's neighbor and family friend. Connie called me that afternoon and asked where I was.

"I'm Christmas shopping," I told her.

"Well," she said, "you just get one of those toys, take it out of the wrapper, and bring it with you."

"Bring it with me for what? What are you talking about?" I asked.

"I've got Glenn here with me," she said. "He walked here all by himself."

That piece of information landed in my ears like a cannon. For a few seconds, I felt dizzy, my chest tight with panic. What do you mean he walked all the way to Gwynn Oak by himself? I asked.

"Well, he did," Connie replied matter-of-factly, then added, almost cheerfully, "And another thing—he learned to use the bathroom today!"

I don't know if she thought that news would soothe me, but at that moment, it only sharpened my panic. I was scared to death.

"Now don't come over here with your foolishness," Connie said firmly. "He's here, he's with me, he's fine. Just come get him. And bring a toy."

A million questions lunged at my sanity as I stood frozen in the store aisle, staring blankly at the shelves. What if he had been run over by a car? What if someone had kidnapped him? What if the police picked him up—and Lord, CPS—what could I possibly have said? What if he'd been attacked by other kids? The questions came in waves: first fear, then guilt, then anger, then more fear.

I hurriedly paid for the items I'd picked up and rushed to the Stokes' house. That morning, I had dressed Glenn for picture day, his little outfit neat and ready. When I finally reached him, I hugged and kissed him, and in that instant all my fears melted away.

That was the first and only time he ever walked home like that. I did give Mr. Sims a piece of my mind for dropping him off without checking if anyone was at the school before driving away. Of course, deep down I knew it wasn't entirely his fault—but someone had to bear the weight of my fear that day. He apologized profusely and continued taking Glenn to school until third grade, when Glenn began catching two buses on his own.

That piece of information landed in my ears like a cannon. For a few seconds, I felt dizzy, my chest tight with panic. What do you mean he walked all the way to Gwynn Oak by himself? I asked.

"Well, he did," Connie replied matter-of-factly, then added, almost cheerfully, "And another thing—he learned to use the bathroom today!"

I don't know if she thought that news would soothe me, but at that moment, it only sharpened my panic. I was scared to death.

"Now don't come over here with your foolishness," Connie said firmly. "He's here, he's with me, he's fine. Just come get him. And bring a toy."

A million questions lunged at my sanity as I stood frozen in the store aisle, staring blankly at the shelves. *What if he had been run over by a car? What if someone had kidnapped him? What if the police picked him up—and Lord, CPS—what could I possibly have said? What if he'd been attacked by other kids?* The questions came in waves: first fear, then guilt, then anger, then more fear.

I hurriedly paid for the items I'd picked up and rushed to the Stokes' house. That morning, I had dressed Glenn for picture day, his little outfit neat and ready. When I finally reached him, I hugged and kissed him, and in that instant all my fears melted away.

That was the first and only time he ever walked home like that. I did give Mr. Sims a piece of my mind for dropping him off without checking if anyone was at the school before driving away. Of course, deep down I knew it wasn't entirely his fault—but someone had to bear the weight of my fear that day. He apologized profusely and continued taking Glenn to school until third grade, when Glenn began catching two buses on his own.

One night, Glenn came home all worked up. He and a friend from school—Michael Sher, whose father, Richard Sher, co-hosted the local Baltimore talk show *People Are Talking* with Oprah Winfrey—had been stopped by a policeman who accused them of speeding. It shook him. He knew the officer had lied, but he also knew the stop had less to do with the number on the speedometer than with the skin he wore. They went to court, and when the officer didn't show up, the case was dismissed.

Another time, while babysitting for a Jewish family whose son was Glenn's classmate, he and Frankie decided to have a small party at the house while the family was out of town. Word spread. Before long, a group of white high school students from the local public school—friends of some Park School kids—showed up. Glenn and Frankie stepped outside, locked the door behind them, and told the boys they weren't invited. One of them had a gun.

I don't know the details of how Glenn managed to defuse the moment, but when he told me about it later, I felt a surge of ice run down my spine. A million things could have gone wrong. While I trusted my boy, I didn't trust the others. In a crowd, it was always easiest to single out the Black boy, to make him the scapegoat.

By the time Glenn was navigating those school hallways, racism had shed its fire hoses and billy clubs. Now it wore khakis and carried policy binders. It smiled at you before it marked you down. It offered a scholarship, then asked if your mother could serve on the diversity committee. It was subtler, not softer. And I was there, watching.

I had walked the road before him, barefoot on ground that cut, while he glided across in polished shoes. When Glenn came home with questions—why his teacher kept overlooking his raised hand, why he got sent to the office for being "disruptive" when all he had done was speak up—I had answers. Or at least comparisons.

In my time, we knew what we were fighting. Signs told us where we could sit. Water fountains declared what we were worth. Now, the signs were invisible—written in zip codes and standardized tests. But I still recognized the language.

Park School had money. And money meant quiet campuses, after-school enrichment, and no crumbling ceilings or broken chalk. It meant opportunity with conditions. They didn't just accept you—you had to pay. And not just in tuition. You had to bring your best-behaved child, the one who could code-switch by instinct and not ruffle feathers. They didn't want your whole child. Just the part that wouldn't challenge the architecture of their comfort.

Still, I felt safer with Glenn there. He didn't have to rely on Daddy to drive him all over the city for sports or music programs like I once did. Everything was on campus. Contained. Curated.

But safety is not sanctuary. And Glenn didn't feel equal. He knew. You can't polish inequality out of an institution with a tuition check. He saw how his white friends were treated—how their complaints became action almost immediately, while his were dismissed as "attitude."

He had a friend, Frankie—another sharp Black boy, raised by good people who understood what it meant to demand better. Frankie stood with him whenever something foul happened. Protested with him. Because they were both raised by folks who didn't take nonsense. Frankie's father, Frank Boston, was a state legislator. So when Glenn and Frankie walked into the headmaster's office, they were not just children. They were *ours*. And the headmaster knew it. He knew exactly whose children they were.

That was the beginning of a new kind of pressure: *You can come in—but you must be better.*

Glenn learned early that the gate would open—but it would never disappear. He learned to walk through it with his back straight and his voice clear, knowing full well that any misstep would be traced back to me. To us. To every Black mother who dared to want more for her child than just survival. And I carried that too. Because even love has weight.

But that's the thing about love: it pushes us to plant seeds in soil we were never allowed to touch, to hope for blooms in gardens we were once barred from entering, and to teach our children how to grow even when the sun plays favorites. Glenn walked that road with both eyes open. He didn't ask to be exceptional. But I asked it of him. Because the world would ask it anyway.

I gave birth to a curious little boy—the kind of curious that asked questions from sunup to sundown, until I rubbed my temples raw trying to keep up. Sometimes I'd run out of patience. That insatiable curiosity, that hunger to understand the world, was present from his earliest days. I thank my lucky stars I didn't end up with twins, like his father, who was one of a set. That curiosity—it was Glenn's gift, though some days it was my trial. But I knew better than to hush it. You never hush the flame in a Black boy. The world will try that soon enough.

You learn a lot about your child if you pay attention in those first two—well, really, I'll say three—formative years. By the time they're three, you pretty much know the direction they're headed. Listening when they make up stories, when they ask how clouds are made, when they stop mid-sentence to stare out the window like they've glimpsed something you can't see. By the time Glenn was three, I had already caught a glimpse of the man inside the boy. And it was my job—not to push him there, but to guide him.

And guidance is an art. You don't grab a child by the hand and drag them to who you want them to be.

One evening at the kitchen table, we were eating, and I said to him, "I know you're a minority at Park School, but you don't have to stay there. Just like I pay tuition there, we can find somewhere else for you. You've got to go to private school because I can't have you in public school and then worry about you while I'm working."

The public schools in Baltimore in the late 1970s and early 1980s were a stark contrast to what I envisioned for my son. They were often underfunded, overcrowded, and disproportionately burdened by systemic inequities that left too many Black students behind. Sending him to Park School was a sacrifice—a constant stretch of my budget—but it was a choice I felt compelled to make for his future.

I told him, "If they're not treating you well, you won't learn. And if you don't learn, you won't be able to grow up, take care of yourself, and become a decent human being. So if you're not happy, you need to let me know."

He got an attitude and said, "I'm not a minority." I thought to myself, "Oh Lord, they've brainwashed my child, and it hasn't even been a year." So I asked him, "If you're not the minority, then who is?" He replied, "The ones who didn't get picked. The ones who aren't at Park School with me."

At that point, I knew he was fine. I didn't need to harp on it. If it didn't bother him, then I didn't need to pay it any mind. Children are curious like that. Dr. Clinton once told me, "When Glenn asks you a question, just answer it truthfully. He'll listen as long as he wants, and when he's heard enough, he'll walk away." And that's exactly what happened one day. He asked me something, and halfway through my answer, he had heard all he needed and just walked off. Dr. Clinton was right—children only want what they need to know, not the whole story.

Later on, around 11th or 12th grade, as he navigated the ever-changing social landscape of high school, Glenn encountered a particularly eye-opening form of racial bias. He had an Asian chemistry teacher who tried to say he had failed the class. But Glenn, being the activist he was, gathered Debbie and his friends together, and they all gave statements. Debbie admitted she never took the final exam. David said he didn't even turn in the final paper. Yet, they had all received B's. Glenn was the only Black student in the class— and the only one being targeted. It was pure racism.

People ask me sometimes, "Was it worth it? That private school tuition, all those sacrifices?" The data speaks for itself. In the 1980–81 school year, Black students made up only about 8% of private school enrollment nationally, reflecting the steep financial and social hurdles for families like ours. All I wanted was to raise an independent Black man. I wanted him to be free. To be whole. To walk through this world as a decent Black man who could think for himself, feed himself, and speak his mind. And I got all that, plus so much more.

I suffered paying for it; those were rough years. I had to make many sacrifices in the process, including losing a house to foreclosure at one point. But hell yes—it was worth it.

Many years later, at one of his racial equity Courageous Conversation Summits, someone asked me if this—his success, his life's work—was what I had wanted for him. I said simply, "I just wanted him to be independent and a good person." He made it out of Baltimore. I guess it's true after all—wildflowers don't care where they grow.

I haven't seen Leroy since shortly after Glenn was born. And for a long time, I used to joke—half-hearted, half-healed—"He could be dead for all I know." It wasn't meant to sound cruel, but I understand now how it did. Still, it was the truth. I had no idea where he was, what he was doing, or who he was with. And to be honest, I didn't care to know. He wasn't showing up. Wasn't contributing. Not financially. Not emotionally. Not even with a phone call. So I stopped pretending his absence was my burden to carry.

There's something that happens to a woman—especially a Black woman—when she realizes the cavalry isn't coming. You stop scanning the horizon. You stop checking your watch. You stop keeping a seat warm at the table. You just get up and fix the damn meal yourself. People talk a lot about *forgiveness* and *reconciliation*, as if they're owed simply because time has passed. But time doesn't heal all wounds—it just teaches you how to walk without limping.

And I learned. I'd already been there myself—I grew up without my biological father in the house. But the difference was, even though he wasn't physically present, my father tried. He reached out. Stayed in touch. He didn't disappear into the folds of convenience or cowardice. So when it came to Leroy, I didn't waste my breath. If a man wants to be part of his child's life, he will. No amount of chasing, reminding, or begging will give him integrity.

I wasn't about to go bankrupt—spiritually or emotionally—trying to collect what wasn't being offered. I didn't call Leroy with updates. Didn't send pictures. Didn't whisper his name to Glenn as though that would keep him alive in his life. Because the truth is, it wouldn't. Glenn had a village around him. My parents—and even my daddy, despite our issues—were there for me during those early years. I took responsibility for myself and my son, working hard to make sure we were taken care of.

And I refused—*refused*—to raise my son on the shallow hope that one day a man who had walked away would suddenly decide to walk back in and fill shoes he'd never even tried on. I made peace with that early. And it was important that I did. Glenn deserved a mother who was present, not one haunted by ghosts. Chasing a man who wasn't chasing us would have only taught my son that love was something you had to beg for. And that was never going to be the story I passed down.

With Glenn at a fair in Canada

4

THE NAMES WE CARRY

I think there is something profoundly revealing about the names we are given and the names we choose—how they shift and settle like sediment in the river of time. Over the course of my eighty-plus years, I have worn many names, each like an ornament for a different ritual: *Colored, Negro, Black, African American.* Each one a reflection not of who I was, but of who America decided I should be at any given moment.

My birth certificate, now yellowed with age, bears the description "colored"—that delicate euphemism white folks used when they wanted to acknowledge our existence without fully confronting what that existence meant. It was 1945, the world still raw from war, and I entered it as a "colored" baby, as if I were something dipped in paint rather than born of flesh and blood and dreams.

Later, around the time Daddy finalized my adoption, the official papers began to read *"Negro."* Then came the movement, the marching, the dreaming—and we became *Black*. There was power in that transformation, power in claiming a word that had once been hurled at us like stones and polishing it until it shone like armor.

The government forms I filled out during my working years bore the label *"Black female,"* and later still, we evolved into *"African-American"—the* hyphenated identity that tried to hold two continents in its embrace. For a brief time, rebellious in my own quiet way, I would check *Other* on official documents and write in *Black* with careful strokes, reclaiming the simplicity of a word that had taught me to stand tall.

But names, I have learned, are only the beginning of the story. My first teacher in the curriculum of race was my grandmother, though she never called it that. She taught me through her hands—what they could and could not touch, where they were welcome and where they were forbidden. "You can look, but don't touch," she would say, her voice carrying the rhythm of a thousand small humiliations. "If you see something pretty, just point at it. But don't lay a hand on it."

Even as a child, I understood that our very touch was considered contamination, that my small brown fingers carried some invisible stain that might rub off on the merchandise. We could look—they allowed us that much—

but touching was illegal, she explained, as if my grandmother's hands, which had sewn finer stitches than anything in that store, were dangerous weapons.

The irony was not lost on me, even then. We were permitted to clean their homes, to touch their children, and to prepare their food with these same hands that were forbidden from caressing a hat or testing the softness of fabric meant for sale. It was my first lesson in the peculiar mathematics of American racism—how proximity was acceptable when it served their needs but became criminal when it suggested equality.

By the time I reached junior high school, the world was shifting beneath our feet like tectonic plates rearranging themselves.

"Janet, do you remember that interview you had to get into junior high school?" Daddy asked me years later, when I was visiting him in the hospital. His memory then was as sharp as a blade, cutting through the comfortable myths I had built around my own story.

"Interview?" I responded, genuinely confused.

"Right after the law was passed. Did you think they just opened their doors to every Black child?" he pressed.

The revelation settled over me like snow, cold and clarifying. I had not simply walked into integration; I had been selected for it, chosen for an experiment to test whether children like me could survive in spaces designed to exclude us. We weren't just students—we were pioneers, though no one had bothered to give us maps for the territory we were being asked to explore.

My best friend's father was a doctor, and that fact felt as natural as sunrise. We lived in row houses that lined the streets like books on a shelf, each family its own story of achievement against odds. Many of those fathers were veterans who had fought for freedom abroad, only to come home and discover they'd have to fight for it again on American soil. The GI Bill had given them the means to buy homes, to carve out neighborhoods where children like me could be treated by doctors who looked like us—like Dr. Redta, the West Indian physician who performed my tonsillectomy in a small pediatric unit that belonged wholly to our community.

This was the world that shaped me—insular, perhaps, but intentionally so. We built our own institutions because we had learned not to depend on the kindness of those who had proven, time and again, that they had none to spare. When it came time for my medical care, I was treated in facilities run by and for people who knew my life had value—not because some law demanded it, but because they could see it reflected in my eyes.

It wasn't until *Brown v. Board* forced me to step beyond the borders of our carefully constructed world that I fully understood what we had built—and why it mattered. Suddenly, I wasn't just a student. I was a symbol. In those new classrooms, every answer I gave—or failed to give—was measured not as Janet's but as a verdict on our people's intelligence, worth, and right to belong. It was never just my desk, my grade, or my presence. It was all of ours.

Years later, when I walked into the Department of Social Security, Daddy reminded me that even this was no accident. "If you don't remember the interview for junior high, I know you remember the interview for your government job," he'd say, his voice always laced with that mix of pride and warning.

I still remember that Saturday morning, standing with my right hand raised, promising to uphold the Constitution of the United States. We were a small group, handpicked by Congressman Parren Mitchell to take up space in a system that had, for so long, locked its doors to us. We weren't just employees—we were foot soldiers in a quiet revolution.

It was a blessing, too, that the Stokes family lived next door. Mr. Stokes was one of the few Black men working in information technology at the time, and he offered me rides from East Baltimore to West Baltimore, where the massive Social Security building loomed like a fortress of bureaucracy. His presence made those drives feel less like exile and more like an expedition—two Black neighbors carving a path into spaces where we had been told we didn't belong.

Daddy had a way of pointing out patterns I would have otherwise missed—threads woven through my life that revealed intention where I had only seen chance. "You weren't just any Black girl," he reminded me often. "You were someone who earned her place." His words taught me that my journey had always been both personal and political, an individual path tied to the larger collective struggle.

So when my son Glenn spoke of wanting to visit Topeka, Kansas, I knew exactly what drew him there. "Brown v. Board of Education?" I asked. "The 50th anniversary?" I went with him, not simply as a witness to commemoration but as someone who had lived the history they were honoring—not on the sidelines, but in the very classrooms where that experiment of American integration was tested.

Looking back, I can see how my childhood was both sheltered and expansive, protective and preparatory. The foundation my grandmother laid—rooted in dignity and unshakable self-respect—had prepared me for battles I could not yet name. The dance lessons, modeling classes, charm school, book clubs, NAACP meetings, Urban League gatherings—all of it was part of an intentional education. It wasn't just about refinement; it was about equipping us to move with grace through a world that would alternately welcome or reject us according to calculations beyond our control.

Taking buses through different neighborhoods exposed me to the geography of inequality. I saw the low-income sections like Cherry Hill and Mt. Winans and the predominantly white enclaves like Dundalk. It became clear that where you lived often determined not only the opportunities available to you but also the very dreams you were allowed to nurture. Sometimes, on Saturdays, Daddy would take me along to union meetings. I'd sit quietly in the back, listening as men and women debated justice and fairness. Those voices, steady and insistent, shaped my understanding of how change comes—through the thoughtful, collective action of people unwilling to accept that things must remain as they have always been.

Those afternoons taught me that learning was not confined to classrooms. Education happened wherever people gathered to make sense of the world and to imagine how it might be made better. Later, Daddy would explain what I had overheard—the intricacies of labor relations, the entanglement of civil rights with everyday life—helping me see that the personal was always political, that my own experiences were threads in a much larger fabric of exclusion and resistance.

Now, having lived through the transformation from Colored to Negro to Black to African-American, I know that names matter less than the spirit that inhabits them. Through every iteration, what remained constant was not what others called us, but what we called ourselves when no one else was listening. We were always more than their categories, always richer, more complex than the simple designations they tried to contain us within.

This little colored baby girl born in 1945 grew into a Black woman who came to understand that identity is not something bestowed by others—it is something claimed for oneself. Each name I carried—Colored, Negro, Black, African-American—was less a definition of me than a mirror of America's shifting conscience. My story was never dependent on their recognition. It was written in the spaces between their words, in the communities we built when they refused us entry, and in the excellence we achieved when they declared us incapable.

And perhaps that is the most important lesson I wish to share with you, dearest gentle reader: our worth was never actually up for debate. Not in the signs that marked our exclusion, not in the laws that sought to contain us, not in the boxes we were forced to check. We were always exactly who we knew ourselves to be—whole, capable, brilliant—waiting patiently for America to catch up to the truth we had carried all along.

A WHOLE NEW WORLD

When I finally began traveling beyond the borders of this country that had shaped me, I carried with me all the stories that had flowed through me over the years. And I was not traveling alone—I was traveling with Glenn, my son, who had already learned to move through the world with an ease I was still discovering. Everywhere we went, Glenn had friends waiting. His schooling, from The Park School to the University of Pennsylvania, had given him something I never had—the opportunity to cross color lines with familiarity and confidence.

By the time we began our journeys together in the late 1990s, Glenn had already been crossing oceans since his first year at Penn, collecting friends like shells on distant shores. Barcelona was my first taste of Europe, my first step onto soil that carried dreams different from the American earth I knew. But even there, we were not tourists stumbling through guidebooks and clutching maps. Pablo was waiting for us. Through Glenn's friendship with Pablo, I tasted what I came to call *the real Spain*—not the Spain packaged neatly for visitors.

Glenn's friendships became bridges, carrying us into the authentic heart of each place. In Paris, Rachid met us at the airport, welcoming us with the kind of warmth usually reserved for family. He took us to Versailles, and as I walked through those gilded halls, I found myself thinking not of

Marie Antoinette, but of how far I had come from the little colored girl who wasn't allowed to touch the merchandise in Stewart's Department Store.

In Amsterdam, Sergio crossed the English Channel just to spend a weekend with us, and I marveled at the casual way these young people treated borders, as though the world truly belonged to them. Glenn had learned early that the earth was wide and welcoming—that there were beaches where people shed not only their clothes but also their inhibitions, where freedom carried a meaning altogether different from the kind we had fought for in the streets of Baltimore.

This was the gift of his generation—the ability to move without the weight of history pressing quite so cripplingly on their shoulders. They had been raised with possibilities we could barely imagine, taught that their passions were worthy of pursuit, and that the world was theirs to explore. Glenn had been part of the Black Onyx Society and other organizations, had learned to be active and engaged, and had been encouraged to follow his curiosity wherever it led. And now, as his mother, I was benefiting from the expansiveness I had once only dared to dream for him.

But it was when we finally made our way to Africa that the deepest currents of my journey revealed themselves. Ethiopia and Ghana—a week and a half in each, but lifetimes of recognition and reckoning compressed into those days. We approached these countries the way we approached all our travels: beginning in the museums, grounding ourselves in history before walking the streets where that history still lived and breathed.

In Ethiopia, we met Askie, who introduced us to Professor Barrack, a scholar who became our private guide to a country that felt both alien and ancestral. He took time away from his own life to show us Ethiopia through eyes that loved it—leading us from restaurants where injera was served with ceremonial care to nightclubs where modern Ethiopia pulsed to ancient rhythms, from the lowlands to the high mountains where baboons chattered and scolded us for intruding on their domain.

I remember sitting among those red-breasted baboons, eating lunch while they carried on their raucous conversations around us, and saying to Glenn, "No wonder we don't feel so good. We're sitting here surrounded by baboons doing their thing, and we're just eating like it's nothing! " It was one of those moments that captured something essential about travel—how it strips away the artificial boundaries we construct, how it forces us to confront the raw truth that we are human animals sharing space on this ancient earth.

Going to Africa, especially Ethiopia, did not change my identity in the way people often expected it to. I had always been Black, and I was going to stay Black. The label "African-American" had never sat comfortably with me anyway—it felt like yet another attempt to hyphenate my existence, to make me something compound when I had always been singular in my understanding of who I was.

Being in Ethiopian villages and on the farms felt natural because I had grown up surrounded by Black people, shaped by a community where faces like mine reflected back everything I needed to know about beauty, intelligence, and worth. The only real difference was language—the musical flow of Amharic replacing the familiar rhythms of Baltimore English. But difference, I had long ago learned, was not the same as distance. These were people who looked like people I had known all my life, like relatives scattered across the diaspora by forces beyond our control.

What struck me most powerfully in Ethiopia was not some mythical return to origins, but the immediacy of human suffering. This was 2012, and AIDS was carving its way through the population like a scythe through wheat. Everywhere we went, there were funerals—little caskets, medium caskets, the physical evidence of lives cut short by a disease that had also devastated communities back home. The professor explained the epidemic with the matter-of-fact tone of someone who had learned to live alongside tragedy, and I absorbed his words the way I had absorbed so many hard truths in my life. You take in what you need to know, you feel what you need to feel, and then you move forward.

But it was in the ancient temples that the spiritual dimension of the journey revealed itself. Standing in a holy place that had been sacred for centuries, I found myself in conversation with a priest about the nature of scripture, about the red letters in our Bibles that mark the words of Christ. When I mentioned this tradition to him, he paused, considering, then said, "One would think the whole book would be written in red."

His words hit me like lightning. Something came over me —a presence, a recognition, a deep knowing I could not name but could not deny. The priest saw it too and felt the shift in the air. "Sit down," he told me gently, and I did, letting whatever it was wash over me for five or ten minutes while Glenn and the professor waited quietly. When it had settled into my bones like medicine, the priest asked, "Are you good to go now?" And I was.

Ghana brought different revelations. We stayed at a resort—more comfortable than our Ethiopian accommodations—and had Samuel as our guide. Samuel, who quickly became like family, took us to Cape Coast and the marketplace with the devotion of someone sharing his most precious treasures. The markets in Ghana, like those in Ethiopia, became my preferred places to shop. I had no patience for the vendors who accosted tourists on the streets. If I wanted something, I would find it in the organized chaos of the markets, where commerce carried dignity, where bargaining was an art, and relationships mattered more than quick profit.

But it was Cape Coast Castle that broke me open in ways

I hadn't expected. That fortress—where my ancestors had been held like cargo, where human beings had been reduced to lines in a ledger—demanded more of me than any museum, market, or mountain climb ever could.

I have photographs of myself standing outside those cell doors, and in every single one, my head is bowed. I couldn't look at the camera, couldn't pretend to be a casual visitor in the face of such concentrated anguish. The stains on the walls told stories no guidebook could capture—blood, urine, and the other remnants of human suffering pressed into stone and mortar, still visible after centuries.

When our guide, Blankson, spoke, I felt my first real encounter with what I would later come to understand as African sensitivity—not some mystical link to ancient roots, but a visceral ability to feel history in the very air of places where history had carved its deepest scars. I didn't need company to process it. I was comfortable being alone with the ghosts, letting them speak what they needed me to know.

Years later, when Glenn was planning the Homecoming trips, I would tell him to give Blankson my love. "That's what his mother named him," I would say. "So that's what people should call him." Names matter. They carry the weight of intention, the love of the people who spoke them first.

When friends asked me to tell them about my Africa experience before they made their own journeys, I always refused. "I can't," I would tell them. "It's got to be your own experience. When you come back, we can talk, but I won't tell you what mine was before you go." Each person has to meet Africa on their own terms, has to allow the continent to reveal itself without the filter of someone else's expectations or interpretations.

I know that for many people, going to Africa changes something fundamental about how they see themselves and how they reintegrate into American society afterward. I believe that transformation depends largely on what they've already experienced in life—what foundation they've built for understanding who they are and where they come from. By the time Glenn was ready to take me, I was eager to go, knowing I would simply be adding new chapters to the education I had already received.

My teachers had prepared me to face the world, had given me African-American history before it was called that, and had grounded me in the knowledge that my roots extended far beyond the borders of America. At Morgan, studying economics and political science, I had learned to see patterns of power and resistance that connected struggles across continents and centuries. I had enough knowledge to understand that my roots were somewhere else, even as I claimed my place in America.

A lot of how people adjust to life in the United States after visiting Africa depends on their experiences here—on what they've already made peace with and what still wounds them. I had been surrounded by adults who were realists—my mother, my grandmother, Daddy, and my teachers. They didn't sugarcoat things or spin fantasies. I didn't grow up on fairy tales—no Cinderella stories to convince me that magic would rescue me from whatever circumstances I faced. Instead, I was introduced to Richard Wright in middle school, discovered James Baldwin soon after, and later expanded my reading to include Toni Morrison and Maya Angelou. These books lived in my house, and I read them at my own pace, with a desire to understand rather than escape.

My mother taught me that if I didn't understand something, I could always find answers in the library, in those card catalog drawers that held the keys to knowledge. "If I can't teach you," she would say, "you can learn there because you have the ability to read." This was how we approached life—with the confidence that understanding was always possible if you were willing to do the work to find it.

So while I have come to terms with being called African-American, it has never sat well with me completely. I use the term because it's the legal definition on most forms now, but honestly, as a retiree, how many forms do I fill out? Not many. I established myself a long time ago, proved what I needed to prove, and earned what I needed to earn.

Whenever I went to the bank to get a loan, the process was straightforward because I had done my research, knew my worth, and understood my position. "I have a house," I told them. "This is what it's worth, and I want to make a loan against it." Aside from the standard procedures, it was as simple as it had been for white folks for years. The bank representative filled out most of the form and handed it to me to review and sign. I haven't had to fill out many forms since I bought my current house sixteen years ago.

Every chance I get, if I have to identify myself, I do. But beyond that—just look at me, and you can see what I am. If I open my mouth, you know what I am. I haven't had problems with racial identification since they introduced the term "African-American." I didn't like it then, and I still prefer to identify as a Black female. If a form doesn't offer a choice between Black and African-American, I'll check African-American. I don't care. It doesn't matter to me at this point in my life.

What matters is the journey itself—the roads I've traveled, the waters I've crossed, and the friendships that have bridged continents and generations. What matters is the knowledge that the world is vast and varied, that there are places where my face fits naturally into the landscape, where my presence is welcomed without question or qualification.

Traveling gave me that gift—the ability to see myself as a citizen of the world rather than a refugee from American racism. It was about escape, yes, but also about expansion—not running from who you are but discovering who else you might be.

And in the end, whether I call myself Colored or Negro or Black or African-American matters less than the truth I carry in my bones: that I am a woman who has crossed waters both literal and metaphorical, who has stood in dungeons and danced in foreign streets, who has tasted injera in Ethiopia and paella in Spain, and who has learned that home is not just a place you come from but a feeling you carry with you wherever you go.

5
THE COURAGE TO CHOOSE YOU

Love, I have learned, is not always the soft thing they write about in romance novels. Sometimes it is a season that arrives disguised as necessity, wearing the mask of companionship when what you really need is a witness to your life—someone to help carry the weight of days that stretch long and demanding before you like unplowed fields.

When I met Perkins at the Social Security Administration in 1966, I was still carrying the sweetness of that Puerto Rican man's kindness on my tongue, still remembering what it felt like to be chosen for joy rather than convenience. Perkins was my colleague, steady as government work itself, and when he asked me to marry him after a year of what we called courting, I said yes with the practical part of my heart that had learned to make peace with good enough.

Mother was happy to see me getting out of the house, away from the restraints Daddy was placing on me as a single mother. "That girl needs to live her own life," she would say, and I knew she was right. At twenty-two, I was tired of being everyone's idea of what a young mother should be—grateful, quiet, content with whatever scraps of independence they were willing to throw my way.

We married in 1967, and I threw myself into the business of being a wife the way I had thrown myself into motherhood—with determination and a willingness to make the best of whatever hand life had dealt me. I could be a wife, I told myself. I had proven I could be a mother; surely I could learn this other dance, this other way of organizing my days around someone else's needs and expectations.

For eighteen years I lived with him; for twenty years I wore his name like a coat that never quite fit right but kept me warm enough. I used to think that proved something—that I wasn't just a single woman who could do whatever she pleased, but someone capable of commitment, of seeing things through even when they stopped feeling like a choice and started feeling like endurance.

Perkins wasn't abusive in the way that leaves bruises you can point to, marks that tell a story everyone can understand. He was abusive in the way that slowly erases you, like water wearing away stone so gradually you don't notice until you look up one day and wonder where you went. He didn't come home some nights, and when he did, he expected what so many Black men expected in those days: a meal waiting, a clean house, and a woman who had spent her day making his life comfortable while her own dreams gathered dust in corners like forgotten furniture.

But see, he was lucky. I had a son to feed, a house to keep, and a life to maintain—whether he showed up or not. Perkins was blessed by my necessity, blessed by the fact that I would have been doing all these things anyway, with or without him. I could have been a lot worse to him than I was.

By the fifth or sixth year of our marriage, I realized he wasn't going to change. He would hang out with his friends, live selfishly, and treat our home like a hotel where he could check in and out at will. That's when I started making my own arrangements, finding my own ways to feel like a woman worth choosing rather than just a wife worth keeping.

I had a colleague at work who helped with Glenn's Cub Scout activities. He'd take me to lunch at nice places downtown and somehow reminded me what it felt like to be seen and appreciated. We became lovers, good friends, and conspirators in the art of living fully despite the constraints of circumstance. My only requirement was to respect Perkins as much as I could while still living the life I needed to live to raise my son properly.

I kept my relationships private and used my government leave to take long lunches and day trips to D.C. I didn't throw it in Perkins's face—that would have been cruel and unnecessary. That was just how I lived, how I survived, and how I maintained my sense of self in a marriage that had become more like a business arrangement than a love story.

They say if you're lucky,, you meet one person in your lifetime who makes your heart beat faster than its rhythm allows. Who makes your stomach churn in a funny way, reddens your cheeks, and leaves your lips struggling not to part sideways? I was fortunate to have this once-in-a-lifetime experience. It was during this period in my marriage to Perkins that I met him. His name was Clarence. Clarence Moore. Even now, decades later, a smile forces its way across my face when I say his name. We met in December of 1983, at a club called Signatures in Baltimore.

He was in the military, my Clarence, and when I first saw him on that dance floor, something in me recognized something in him. That moment when you meet someone and the world shifts slightly on its axis, and you notice the light falls differently afterward—that's what happened when our eyes met across that crowded room.

It was the way Clarence treated me, perhaps, that made me know I had come to my own reckoning with this famous, sacred feeling. He was funny, gentle, and every time I thought of him, I felt like I had found my own Tea Cake from *Their Eyes Were Watching God*. He had this thick West African accent. When I think back on those two years he was stationed here, I remember how romance felt like breathing—natural and necessary.

He was teaching at Morgan, and I recall visiting him there one day, surprising him at work. In his melodic accent, surprised but still trying to maintain professionalism, he scolded me: "What are you doing here? You know this is a professional environment." But even in his surprise, there was tenderness. "Why don't I see you this evening at my place?" he said.

But love, as I have come to learn, can be as fragile as morning dew. After two years, the military moved him away, and Baltimore was never his home to begin with. The leaving was hard. I went to Fort Meade to see him, clinging to what remained of us, but by New Year's Eve 1986, when I called to wish him well, a woman's voice answered his phone. "You have the wrong number," she said. And in those words, I heard the final closing of a door I hadn't even known was shutting. He moved from the apartment he had been assigned.

He never called after that. His forty years of military service would have been completed in 2024, and sometimes I wonder if he's still out there somewhere—if he ever thinks of those two years in Baltimore, of me.

The not knowing sits differently now than it did then. Time has a way of softening even the sharpest edges of loss, and what once felt like abandonment now feels more like the natural flow of lives moving in different directions. But that gift—the knowing of what it feels like to love another deeply, in a romantic way—I still hold sacred.

My mama was the only one who ever knew about him and the only witness to what bloomed between us.

I could have left Perkins earlier, but my attorney advised me to wait. "Just sit down for two years; you'll leave him," he said. We were already in the eighteenth year of our marriage. When the time came that I couldn't take it anymore, I sat Perkins down and told him the truth with the kind of clarity that comes when you've finally reached the end of your rope.

"You don't go anywhere with me," I said. "You contribute very little to my life and Glenn's life. If it wasn't for me having the job I had, we wouldn't have had half of what we had." The words came out calm and factual—not angry, just true.

That morning—oh, I remember it so clearly—I was driving to work, bone-tired of Perkins and his nonsense. That man would come home late, eat whatever I had prepared, fall into bed, and be gone again before sunrise, with barely a word exchanged between us. I had given him every opportunity to do better, to step up as a partner, but it was clear he wasn't going to change.

And while it frustrated me, I paused and reminded myself, "Now don't be a fool, girl. You've been taking care of yourself and holding this family together. You can keep doing it."

But that morning, something shifted in me like tectonic plates rearranging themselves beneath the earth. Then I spotted it—a big sign by the road that read: "Three-Month

Trial Rent. No Contract." It felt like the universe was speaking directly to me, offering a way out I hadn't even known I was looking for.

Before I even clocked in at work, I pulled into that apartment complex, marched into the leasing office, and filled out the paperwork for a one-bedroom trial rental. I didn't hesitate. I didn't second-guess myself. I went to work that day feeling like I had taken the first step toward reclaiming my life, like I had finally remembered I was more than just someone's wife, someone's convenience.

A few days later, they called. "We've got a one-bedroom available for you," the voice said, and relief washed over me like cool water on a hot day. "Perfect," I replied. "I'll take it." From that moment, my mind was made up. I was leaving.

That evening, Perkins came home as usual, and I cooked dinner, but it wasn't the kind of warm, welcoming meal I used to prepare. I cooked just enough for the house, but I didn't leave anything out for him. That was my small act of rebellion, my quiet way of saying the days of automatic service were ending.

When the day finally came, I didn't make a scene. I packed my personal belongings into one of those big green trash bags and grabbed only what I absolutely needed. It was the start of summer when I moved into that one-bedroom apartment, and I didn't even have enough money to put gas in my car. The complex had a shuttle van, so I rode that back and forth to work while my mother helped me with food. All I had to my name was my next paycheck.

That first night, I unrolled Glenn's old sleeping bag on the floor and made my bed there. It wasn't much, but it was mine, and that meant everything. Later, my mother mentioned a furniture sale at the fairgrounds, and we went together. I bought the basics—a bed frame and a tiny café table with two chairs. No couch, no dresser, no frills. Just what I needed to sleep, eat, and begin again.

I spent the next couple of years in that apartment making it work, finding my rhythm as a woman who had chosen herself over convenience, who had decided her worth was not measured by how much she could endure of what someone else was willing to dish out. I walked a little taller, knowing I had taken control of my life.

My attorney had been strategic about the timing. "Janet, you're head of the household," he told me. "You've got things in order. Don't get it twisted—it's good for you. I can see it in you, and it's good for your son too." He wanted me to stay legally married for twenty years because Perkins was a veteran, and the rules around spousal benefits might work in my favor later.

"You want your divorce now, but it's going to take a couple of years," he explained. "Perkins is a veteran, and you never know when the rules might change. Even though you've already arranged your burial plot and funeral plans, you need to hold out." He was determined that I make it to a twenty-year marriage, whether I liked it or not.

We married in '67, I left him in '85, and I divorced him in '87. Only because, as my attorney said, "You're going to be married to him for twenty years since he's a veteran." At the time, if you didn't remarry and your spouse was eligible for Social Security, you could collect it too. My attorney, Jewish and wise in the ways of protecting women's interests, was adamant that I settle down, make myself content, and carry on with my life.

When I left Perkins, I had nothing but my next government check coming in two weeks. But I had something more valuable than money—I had my dignity back, my self-determination, my understanding that I was worth more than a marriage built on habit and convenience.

Perkins made the mistake of not filing for legal separation properly. He thought that with my salary, he could seek separation and even tried to ask for alimony—as if he had lost something, when I had been the one doing all the giving. That's when I knew it was time to take a firm stand.

My lawyer and his were locked in a stalemate because the disparity in our salaries would only work in my favor. I made it clear I wasn't paying him a dime, and I felt vindicated when my lawyer echoed that sentiment. "If he had a bit more money, I'd go after him," he said, "but you're not going to waste resources on someone who isn't worth it."

For nearly a decade after our divorce, Perkins didn't

speak to me. If we happened to land at the same friend's house, he'd leave the minute I walked in. I didn't care. I was there to visit, not to nurse his wounded pride or carry the weight of his discomfort with choices I had every right to make.

People sometimes misunderstand my story. They think I used Perkins to get Glenn where he is. But what part of my journey did they miss? I made the money. I supported my family. I wasn't selfish with it. Every decision I made was for us to grow as a family—even when "us" didn't really include a husband who was present.

When I finally got my driver's license, I took Glenn to meet his natural grandfather, my biological father. I even invited Perkins along. He came, and while he and my father got along well enough, it didn't deepen our relationship—or theirs. Later, Glenn mentioned how limited his connection with his grandfather felt, and I reminded him: at least he got to meet him, hear his stories, and spend some time together. Not everyone gets that chance.

The relationship I had with my biological father wasn't conventional, but it was enough for me to make peace with it. When he was facing heart surgery, I didn't hesitate. I went to Philadelphia and stayed through it all. To me, it wasn't about whether he had been present in my life or not. I knew the reasons why our relationship was the way it was, and when the time came, I did what I felt was required of me as his daughter.

Life doesn't always give you the chance to go back and fix things. When you realize that, you have to start where you are today and do the work. Don't just talk about it—do it. That's been my guiding principle. I've come this far by faith, trusting in something bigger than me to carry me through, but I don't just sit around praying and waiting for things to happen. I get up, I take action, and I leave the rest in God's hands.

There's a balance, though. Sometimes I realize I'm digging too deep, trying to change the plan instead of following it, and that's when I know I have to step back, leave it with God, and move on. There's always more I could be doing with the time I have left, and I intend to keep going as long as I can.

My marriage to Perkins was like a house I lived in but never truly inhabited. I kept it clean, maintained its structures, and made sure it functioned properly, but it was never really home. Home, I learned, is not a place you stay because it's convenient or expected. Home is where you can be yourself fully, where your presence is valued rather than just tolerated, and where love is offered freely rather than earned through service. He and Glenn never had a smooth relationship, and many years later Glenn would say to me, "I'm just so glad he didn't legally adopt me."

That little apartment with its bare floors and modest furniture became more of a home to me than the house I had shared with Perkins for eighteen years. It was a sanctuary, a reminder that sometimes the biggest changes start with one small, bold step toward the life you actually want rather than the life you think you're supposed to accept.

And perhaps that is the most important lesson of all—that we are never too old, never too set in our ways, never too defined by our circumstances to choose ourselves, to remember our worth, to walk away from situations that diminish us rather than celebrate us. The house I built with Perkins served its purpose for a season, but when that season ended, I had the courage to leave it behind and build something new, something that was truly mine.

6

IN SERVICE OF THE UNSEEN

Some folks are born knowing what they're meant to do in this world, like seeds that carry their own instructions for growing. Others, like me, have to learn their purpose through the calloused hands of their grandmothers, through watching how tenderness can be practical and how service can be its own form of revolution.

I watched my Granny take care of her elderly clients with the kind of devotion that never made the newspapers but kept the world spinning on its axis. Her hands moved like prayers over fragile bodies, and her voice carried the authority of someone who understood that dignity was not a luxury but a birthright. Perhaps it was from watching her work diligently, providing care to others, that my own dream of becoming a social worker began to take root.

That had been my dream all along, though perhaps I

would have dreamed of something else if I had grown up under different circumstances. Our people were only just learning to dream big dreams in those days. Even Martin Luther King Jr. could only dream, at that point, that one day a Black man would rule America—a dream that may have sounded funny to some folks, perhaps even foolish. But dreams are free, so he dreamed anyway, and that freedom gave the rest of us permission to reach beyond what seemed possible.

At fourteen, I became what they called a "pinky"—my uniform had a pink stripe with a little apron that marked me as someone learning to take care of people. This was in an all-Black hospital. It was me and two other girlfriends. I did that work for about two years, from fourteen to sixteen, and at the same time, I was volunteering with the local chapter of the NAACP. For me, caring for individuals and fighting for justice were two sides of the same coin. Working at that hospital was a way to keep us busy and out of trouble, but more than that—it was where the seed of my calling first pushed through the soil of possibility.

When I had Glenn at nineteen, Wesley got me a job at a Black-owned and operated pharmacy. Wesley was already working there, delivering medicine on a bicycle with a basket full of pharmaceutical bags, riding through the night without anyone robbing or hurting him—because even in those dangerous streets, folks understood that some work was sacred and some missions couldn't be interrupted.

After my six-week checkup with my OBGYN—who had gone to school with my mother, because that's how tight our community was—Wesley told me to go across the street and see Charlie Burns, who might have a job for me. I went, and Charlie hired me on the spot, though he told me he could only keep me at the main pharmacy temporarily because they sold alcohol and I was just nineteen. But he had another store in East Baltimore where they didn't sell alcohol, so he said, *"If you still want a job, show up there on Monday at noon."*

I did, and I worked the night shift, from noon to eleven. That pharmacy had Black pharmacists, so I was still with my people, still in the embrace of a community that understood that work was dignity and dignity was survival. I worked there for about a year, starting when Glenn was seven weeks old, still learning to balance the scales of new motherhood with the necessity of making a living.

In December 1965, I transitioned to work for the federal government at the Social Security Administration, beginning my lifelong career of service to the country. Even this, I'd later come to learn, was because a group of us had been hand-picked based on our family lifestyle, test scores, and grades. When I first walked into that Social Security building, my heart was heavy with the encumbrance of girlhood dreams deferred. Life, in her mysterious way, had other plans. She set me down at a desk piled high with manila folders and said, *"Child, this is your ministry now."* And what a ministry it became.

I had finished two years of college when I had Glenn, and if it hadn't been for Congressman Parren Mitchell keeping an eye on things, they probably would have kept me at grade two or three forever. But I got promoted to grades two, three, five, seven, eight, and nine in consecutive years—climbing that ladder like it was my personal mountain to conquer.

When I reached grade seven, I entered a career-ladder position that could take me from grade nine to eleven if I passed my evaluations. No problem for me—I had been taking tests and proving myself my whole life. They kept us in training for a year because I worked in disability operations, handling claims for people whose bodies had betrayed them, people who needed someone to stand between them and a system that could be as cold as winter wind.

Retirement claims were handled by the different Program Service Centers, but disability claims were processed in Woodlawn, Maryland, at the central office. When Disability Insurance Beneficiaries (DIB) turned sixty-two, they were automatically converted to retirement benefits if eligible. The opportunities were there like fruit on a tree—I just had to decide what I wanted to pick. I liked disability claims operations, so that's where I planted myself and grew roots. I got promotions each year until I hit that career ladder, and that's when management realized something that should have been obvious from the start: *"She talks a lot. She's going to tell us what's on her mind."* And honey, I sure did.

There was a time when one of those policy-shifting situations arose, like they always do in legal America. Folks were claiming pain as their primary diagnosis, and they had to be considered for disability claims. I was part of a study group to address the issue. Those early days of training were like being baptized in complexity. They rotated doctors through our classroom like seasons, teaching us the intricate language of the human body's failures and endurances. The respiratory system one week, the musculoskeletal the next—each lesson a new way to understand how pain announces itself, how disability declares its presence.

And there, in that summer of learning, I met Carolyn—a white girl from Chicago with eyes that saw past color to competence, past difference to dedication. We became unlikely sisters in that Baltimore training ground, sharing knowledge and laughter in equal measure.

There were days when they'd put me at a desk, a veritable mountain of cases piled high, and and I felt no tremor of fear. The year of rigorous training had forged a quiet confidence within me. I had learned enough to know that if a question arose in a claim I was processing, I could simply walk across those polished floors to the medical division and summon a doctor—a true expert—to provide clarity. By the time I reached Grade 11, a significant rung on the bureaucratic ladder, I was flying through the work with an unerring swiftness, bringing each case to its rightful conclusion.

To find oneself in the embrace of work—truly doing

something for the very fabric of this vast, often indifferent country—was, for me, an unfolding of purpose. I remember telling my colleague Dave once, a man whose steady presence was a comfort in the labyrinthine corridors of the Social Security Administration, that in my girlhood, a lifetime ago, I had envisioned myself as a social worker. And here I was, decades later, performing a similar alchemy, albeit without the intimate, often raw personal exchanges. Yet the human element, with its raw edges of desperation and hope, still found its way to me sometimes. Like when I'd receive calls from the security guard in the lobby about claimants whose faces were etched with frustration, carrying grievances over benefits withheld or misunderstood. I'd go down there and painstakingly explain why their sustenance had been granted or denied. It was not, by official designation, social work, but in the quiet, undeniable pull of its essence, it felt like nothing less.

I had to tell one of my managers straight out one time: "I come here to work to make money because Glenn went from measles to mumps to chickenpox in rapid succession." That boy was sick with everything childhood could throw at him, and every time I took him back for his follow-up with Dr. Clinton, he'd tell me Glenn had caught something else. So I had to take leave, whether I had it saved up or not, because some things are more important than perfect attendance records.

When I went back to work, the manager called me into

his office and said, "You know, we're having trouble promoting you because you don't have any leave left." I looked at him and said, "Well, maybe now it's time for me to tell you—I'm a mother first. And this is the first time anyone has said anything to me about using my leave to take care of my child, but I'll tell you all now: I'm a mother first, and this job comes second."

I've always felt like I could find another job if I needed to. If I wasn't making it here, I'd make it somewhere else. I'd had the job at the pharmacy and had worked at a department store downtown for three months before the government called me. I didn't leave jobs just to leave—I left when better opportunities presented themselves, because I had a child to raise and no time to waste on situations that didn't serve our future.

So I told that manager, "You think I'm here for this job? No. I'm here to make money and take care of my family." I was married to Perkins at the time, but the white folks had a problem with my priorities. They'd say, "But you're married," as if that should change everything. And I'd respond, "So what? You have the luxury of letting your wives stay home. I don't have that luxury."

We spent that whole summer learning everything—processing pay, eligibility, payments, and determinations. During that period, Social Security got involved in a court case, and the commissioner called for me and eight others. One of the managers, a white woman, questioned where I had been with the kind of condescension that implied I needed her approval to move around, saying, "Janet, where have you been?"

I said, "I've been upstairs talking to legal."

She had the nerve to reply, "Well, that's what I heard."

And I looked right at her and said, "You didn't have to hear it. All you had to do was wait 'til I came back downstairs."

These people stayed in their little administrative offices on the top floor—they didn't get involved in the day-to-day operations. I had been sitting with the legal team, unpacking some legal questions about a claim I was processing. Just because something had been done a certain way didn't mean it was the right way. And I told her, "Remember, we're in court because y'all didn't do it the right way!"

In an attempt to get a lick back at me, this woman—this embodiment of bureaucratic arrogance—pushed a colossal postal tub filled to the brim with punch cards to my desk. I will never forget the sight of it. She thought she was punishing me, but all I saw in front of me was a physical manifestation of their incompetence, born from centuries of a warped mindset that others had to do the hard work while they waltzed around with their silky pale skin and cracked the whip.

There were over ten thousand mental health cases unprocessed, and the courts, with their unyielding demands, required every single one to be reviewed. My response was a shrug, a quiet defiance. I said, "Yeah, well, that sounds about right. You all have been after me for a long time. Guess what? I'll take this on too."

Her miscalculation, like so many before her, was forgetting my background in operations—the very mechanics of the system. I called Jack over in systems and told him what was happening. Jack said, "Don't worry, Janet, I'll send my clerks over to get that tub."

I took a little break and crossed the street to meet Jack in systems. He asked me what items they needed to look for to determine if the claims had been reviewed. So I broke it down: every punch card represented a form we used for determinations. "We need to identify which claims actually need to be reviewed. The court doesn't know which ones need attention; they just have numbers." Jack knew exactly what to do.

We pinpointed the items on the 833 form that indicated whether a case had been reviewed. That helped us segregate the mental health cases that truly needed review. By the time I was done, out of those ten thousand claims, only about four thousand still needed to be reviewed.

When I got back to my base, I was working with my colleague Tom. He asked, "Did you actually go over there and reduce the number of claims from ten thousand to four thousand?"

I said, "I most certainly did."

He looked at me like I was a Dahomey Amazon, and I said

to him, "All you need to know is what you're doing. I've been in disability claims for how long? I should know, or I shouldn't have a job here."

He chuckled and said, "Well, that's true."

Those four thousand claims were eventually sent down to my office. I remember telling my friend Carolyn, "See this big canvas tub they pushed up here? That's supposed to be my mental health cases," Carolyn said. "Yup, that's yours."

I sorted the files and sent them out to the different modules responsible for handling claims from various states. We worked geographically. So once I reduced the numbers, the files went to the appropriate teams. It took about two years to finally clear that backlog—two years of people's hopes hanging on the line, finally resolved.

Dave and the men I worked with respected me for that. I was fortunate to work mostly with men. I could talk to them however I wanted. But there was one white woman, Maxine Barshop. I wanted to hang her by her ankles! She was the type who rode her way to the top, if you know what I mean. She came in, skipped all the processes, and became a manager. Next thing we knew, she was a grade 15 director, so you couldn't tell her anything. A Jewish woman, always giving me a hard time. I had to keep reminding myself not to let her get me fired.

One day, she said something to me, and I was mad. I was fussing, and she came out of her office and asked, "Do you have a problem?" I said, "Yes, I do. Let's go to your office and talk about it." She never expected that. Afterward, my friend Fred said, "Janet, you've got the balls of a man." I told him, "That's why I prefer working with men. They don't try to mess with me like the women do."

Maxine, though—she'd mess with me. But she knew she needed me to get the job done. I knew I was the best analyst she had. She was the director, sure, but she didn't know how to do my job. I wasn't going to let her push me around. I had my name on the cover sheet, so I was the one responsible. She never did the job herself, so why was she trying to interfere?

The men—Tom and Dave—didn't question me. If they had a messed-up claim, they'd hand it to me and leave me alone. They knew I'd fix it. And if they didn't hear from me for a few days, they didn't bug me—because they understood it didn't get messed up in a day, and it wouldn't get fixed in one, either.

That was my personal Social Security motto: *right person, right amount, right time.* So when I saw something wrong, I spoke up without hesitation. I was the analyst—I had worked every part of the operation. The directors? They were just sitting in meetings, often with no idea what was actually happening on the ground where the real work got done.

The irony wasn't lost on me—here I was, doing the work of social service without the social part, helping people I would never see, whose faces would remain forever unknown to me. Yet in every file that crossed my desk, I could feel their breathing. In every medical report, I could hear their sighing. These were America's forgotten children—grown now, broken now, needing now—and I was their unseen angel, their paper advocate, their bureaucratic balm.

I was privileged to work mostly with men who could handle my directness. But the women? Oh, we went head-to-head like prizefighters in a ring. One of them—and you guessed right—would always remind me, "Well, I studied journalism in college," as if that credential gave her some special authority. I'd respond, "So what? What does that have to do with this memo I just gave you? It's technically correct, so leave it alone."

She'd try to make everything fancy, but this wasn't the place for flowery writing. We had specific formats for letters, and we had to fill them with information that would help beneficiaries understand why they were—or weren't—getting what they requested. Clarity was kindness; confusion was cruelty.

One time, she handed me a case that came directly from the commissioner's office, and I asked, "If you know so much, why did you give this to me?" She was trying to set me up for failure, but I wasn't having it. I told her, "Don't try to fix this. You don't have the technical background for it." She didn't know what she was doing—just sitting there collecting that grade fifteen salary while I did the actual work. Yeah, I was pissed.

That's what truly annoyed me—they were making grade

fifteen money while I was at grade eleven doing the complex analysis, cleaning up their mistakes, and solving the problems they created through ignorance or carelessness. At my retirement party, Dave got up in front of 250 people and announced that I wasn't very cooperative. I said, "You don't tell 250 people that!" But he asked, "Well, were you?"

I didn't cooperate with grade fifteens much; that's true. I was too busy cleaning up their messes, being sent to different divisions when they got in trouble, and fixing what they had broken through incompetence or indifference. I worked in all five divisions before I retired, like a troubleshooter for human dignity.

One day, senior director Myra came to me and asked, "Janet, what do you want?"

I said, "Nothing in here."

She pressed, "Janet, there's got to be something!"

I said, "I don't want management. I'm already an analyst, and there's nothing in this place that I want."

When she kept pushing, I told her the truth: "You really want to know what I want? I'll be fifty-five in February. I want to retire."

She said, "Well, I can't help you with that."

And I said, "Yeah, I know you can't, but watch me."

When people ask about my biggest achievement during those years, I'd say reaching grade twelve. They didn't want to keep promoting me—a Black woman who spoke her mind and put beneficiaries before bureaucracy—but I got there anyway, climbing that ladder rung by rung, evaluation by evaluation, year by year.

I already knew the game. They watched us like hawks and moved us like pawns. And no matter how many tests we aced or how many exams we passed, they promoted me with one hand while holding me back with the other—always trying to keep me at grade eleven, like it was the ceiling for my kind. But I kept rising. Kept pushing. Because I already knew by then that I was not made for ceilings.

When I think deeply, I understand that my time at Social Security was more than just a career—it was a calling disguised as government work. Every claim I processed, every beneficiary I helped, every time I stood up to management on behalf of someone who couldn't advocate for themselves, I was continuing the work that began when I watched my Granny's hands move with such tenderness over people who needed care.

That social work dream I'd carried since childhood didn't disappear when I took the government job—it transformed, grew larger, and became systemic. Instead of helping one family at a time, I was part of a system that could help thousands, and I was determined to make sure that system worked the way it was supposed to work—with compassion, competence, and an unwavering commitment to doing right by the people who needed us most.

On March 1, 2000, I finally retired from the service of these United States, but the truth is, I never really stopped serving. Social Security turned out to be perfect for me after all—it scratched that social work itch I'd carried since I was a girl watching my Granny's healing hands. At my retirement party, Dave Ditman stood up in front of everyone and said, "If I don't remember anything else about Janet, I know this: no matter how stupid our decisions were as directors, Janet was going to do the right thing for the beneficiary, not for us. She didn't care about pleasing us."

He continued, "I had plenty of chances to get corrected by her, even though I was a director. She'd tell me straight up, "That's not going to work." He was in grade fifteen, I was in grade eleven, but I still spoke truth to power whenever I saw something that wouldn't serve the people we were supposed to help. I'd say, "That's not going to work for the beneficiary. I'm here to make sure the right person gets the right amount of money at the right time."

Perkins was still in grade three when we got married, and he didn't reach grades four and five until years later. I even had to fill out his applications for promotions, seeing the grade four postings on the board and saying, "You should apply for this. You might get picked up." And he did, but slowly, without the fire that burned in me to climb as high as the system would allow.

He was ten years older than me, a Korean War veteran with his own way of moving through the world. But when we both retired, I was at grade twelve, and he was at grade five.

7
A DIAMOND OF THE SUN

My grandmother moved through her days with a kind of temporal fearlessness that I have come to understand was not ignorance of mortality but intimate familiarity with it—the way someone who has lived through enough endings learns to hold beginnings more lightly. She never spoke of aging as something to be feared or fought against and never treated the accumulation of years as anything more significant than the accumulation of seasons.

There was never much talk of aging in my family. Not in the way folks speak of it now, like a countdown or a diagnosis, like it's something to dread, fear, or reverse. No creams. No complaints. No lamentations over birthdays. The absence of age-consciousness in our household was not denial but wisdom—wisdom born from generations who had learned that survival depended on understanding what mattered and what did not. We knew, with the certainty that comes from watching too many people disappear too early, that two things were guaranteed in this life: we would be born, and we would die—and everything meaningful happened in the space between those certainties. My Uncle Charlie's prayer—"Lord, I'm not ready to come yet"—was not a plea but a a negotiation, the kind of conversation you have with mortality when you understand it as a neighbor rather than an enemy.

My grandmother never spoke of getting old. Not once do I recall her naming her aches or counting her years aloud. And maybe that's because she knew something the rest of the world hadn't yet figured out—that age is not the enemy. That wrinkles are not warnings. That each line on a Black woman's face is a signature in the Book of Survival.

To be called an eighty-year-old Black woman in America means you have carried within your body the entire sweep of a nation's moral evolution—to have lived through the transformation of a country that began by denying your humanity and has grudgingly, slowly, and incompletely moved toward recognizing it. I have been alive for nearly a century of American time, which means I have witnessed the death of Jim Crow and the birth of the internet, have seen Black children walk into previously all-white schools under military escort, and watched a Black man take the oath of office as President of the United States. I have been called colored, Negro, Black, and African-American. My body has been an archive and a witness, a repository and a testimony to changes that once seemed impossible but proved merely inevitable, given enough time and enough people willing to push against the force of history.

The pre–civil rights era was not background music to my childhood but the very air I breathed, the water I drank, and the ground I walked on every day. The courage required for such living was not extraordinary but ordinary—the daily courage of getting up each morning and deciding to remain human in a world that preferred you less than human; you have the courage of believing in your own possibilities when everything around you suggested they did not exist.

But perhaps the deepest courage was required not for surviving the world as it was, but for raising a Black boy in that world—for nurturing his dreams while preparing him for nightmares he should never have to face, for teaching him to be proud of who he was while keeping him safe from those who would harm him for being exactly that. Glenn represents not just my success as a mother but my success as a revolutionary, proof that love could indeed conquer systems designed to destroy what I loved most. Every day he walks through this world as a whole, educated, confident Black man is a day that validates every sacrifice I made, every risk I took, and every moment I chose to fight rather than surrender.

So when I see Glenn's face tighten with worry as he

watches me navigate my eightieth year—when I witness his anxiety about my aging as though it were a catastrophe rather than an achievement—I find myself asking where this fear originated, because it did not come from the soil that grew me. In the world that shaped me, reaching old age was a triumph, not a tragedy, particularly for a Black woman born when this country still debated whether I possessed a soul worth saving or a mind worth educating. Every year I have claimed has been a small victory against systems designed to ensure I would not live long enough to claim them. Every birthday has been a quiet revolution against expectations that I would not survive childhood, would not escape the violence of poverty, and would not transcend the limitations others tried to place on my dreams. But I also see reflected in his worry the success of my mothering: he loves me deeply enough to fear losing me and has learned to value what I represent in his life strongly enough that the thought of my absence creates anxiety.

That is not to say age does not come with its own challenges. And I think it is the unpreparedness for these challenges that makes many miss the bright side of aging—that it is, in fact, a blessing.

When I discovered my grandmother living in the cramped attic of my uncle's house, relegated to the forgotten spaces while he occupied the comfort below, I felt something ancient and fierce rise within me—the same protective instinct bred into Black women across generations. It was the understanding that sometimes love requires action that cannot wait for permission or discussion. I went and got her without ceremony and brought her to live with me because that is what families do when families remember what family means—when they understand that care flows upward as naturally as it flows down, and that the woman who raised you deserves better than an attic room and benign neglect disguised as accommodation.

It was simply the knowledge that she had given me life in more ways than biology could account for, and now life was asking me to return the gift in whatever measure I could provide. When her mobility began to fail and I could no longer manage her care alone, I found a woman from our church to help. After the cancer diagnosis, I would ask how she was feeling, and she would tell me she was praying for her knees to work that day so she could walk—reducing the entire complexity of illness to the simple request for one day's mobility. *"Let go and let God"* was my grandmother's theology and her daily lived philosophy, an accumulation of decades spent learning that some battles belong to forces larger than human will or worry can command.

We had just celebrated the New Year of 1979 when she became critically ill from the cancer, a diagnosis that had come only the year before. The sickness had eaten deep into her body. One morning—a Wednesday—she asked to be discharged, saying she was tired of staying in a hospital bed. So I took her home that day. By Thursday the situation worsened, and I took her back to the hospital. That Friday evening, I went home to gather fresh supplies and clothing for her. It would be the last time I saw her alive. She joined her ancestors that night—Friday, January 19, 1979.

Her daughter, my mother, was a force who moved through life on her own terms, even when those terms defied logic and sometimes even the safety of everyone around her. She understood the importance of physical health with absolute clarity—our pediatric visits were scheduled with military precision, transitions to adult physicians were seamless, vaccinations were current, and ailments were addressed before they became emergencies. But when it came to her own mental health—the electrical storms in her head that sometimes transformed her into someone we barely recognized—she was as dismissive as a child refusing breastmilk. "Nobody's messing with my head," she would declare, as though treatment for mental illness were an intrusion into the most private aspect of her being.

It was not until she was forty-three years old—after Wendell's birth triggered her second crisis—that a doctor at Spring Grove looked at her records from Crownsville and said, "I think she's bipolar." Ten years of wrong medication, wrong treatments, and wrong understanding of what was happening inside her brain. Ten years of watching her cycle through episodes that left us all walking on eggshells, never knowing which version of our mother would greet us when we came home.

I had spent twelve years volunteering with the National Alliance on Mental Illness,, and that became my graduate education in understanding mental health—listening to parents whose adult children lived with disabilities that made every day a negotiation and learning the language of advocacy. The first time I had to have her committed, Daddy couldn't do it himself. He said, "I can't face a judge and have her committed." And I heard myself responding, "Then I'll do it." Standing before that judge, convincing him that the police needed to pick up my mother and take her to a psychiatric institution, was a kind of responsibility no one prepares you for—the terrible mathematics of love that sometimes requires you to become the person your loved one will hate in order to become the person who saves their life.

She felt betrayed, and she let me have it. "You put me in this place," she said, her voice carrying accusations that cut deeper than any physical wound. And I answered, "I had to—you were going to hurt yourself or somebody else."

When I arrived at her hearing, Wesley was already there. As the double doors opened to let me into the courtroom, I heard her voice before I saw her face: "Look at her. Here she comes. Oh, she thinks she's something." And the terrible thing was that I did think I was something that day. I had chosen one of my favorite outfits, dressed up, and walked into that courtroom knowing that my appearance would be judged along with my testimony. So yes, I was something.

Wesley grabbed me as I walked down the hallway and

said, "Boo, doesn't that sound like Momma?" And I told him, "Oh, I know it. You see, I haven't said a word, but I'm half-tempted to keep her in here all day just for messing with me." We both laughed about it.

I was already a mother myself at this point and had accepted the long-held tradition that our hands were built to provide care—the hands of Black women, carrying the sacred burden of being the ones people call when situations become impossible to manage alone. When my mother's illness made it unsafe for Wendell to stay with her, he came to live with me, my husband, and Glenn. We made it work because that was what needed to happen, with my grandmother helping when she could, despite her own advancing age, staying with us during night shifts.

My volunteer work became professional development almost by accident—moving from the local mental health center to the state advisory board to the federal level—but also because I was genuinely interested in mental health advocacy. This prepared me to handle my mother's care with a knowledge that most family members never acquire. One day she went into crisis and assumed she would return to Spring Grove. I said to her, *"Not this time, Mama. You're going to Sheppard Pratt."* When she asked how I had managed that, I explained that serving on the state advisory board had taught me which hospitals provided better care, and it had given me contacts who could ensure she received treatment in a facility that would see her as a person rather than just another Black woman having a mental health crisis.

To white folks, choosing your psychiatric hospital was nothing special. But for us, it represented access to quality care that had been denied to Black patients for generations—the difference between being warehoused and being treated, between receiving medication that might actually help and being subjected to treatments designed more to control than to heal. When they kept her for a month instead of the expected seventy-two hours, she wasn't happy about the extended stay. But Wesley reported after visiting her that she admitted this place was better than the others, and I felt a complicated satisfaction knowing that my advocacy work had translated into better care for the person who mattered most.

Finding Dr. Del Cruz—who was willing to administer her medication through monthly injections—solved the problem that had made her previous treatments ineffective: her refusal to take pills consistently, her tendency to decide she no longer needed medication just as her symptoms began to improve, and her ability to convince herself that the medications were the problem rather than the solution. "I can't let her get under my skin," I told him during one of our consultations. "I learned that a long time ago when I first started volunteering at the neighborhood mental health center. If I let her make me mad, I'd mess up her treatment like nobody's business."

Wesley would laugh when I explained my approach to managing our mother's condition and her personality simultaneously: "She's always talking about me, but you know what? It just lets me know how much she loves me. Because when she's in crisis, and she can't control what's going on with her, she knows there's one person who'll always watch out for her. And that's me." This was not delusion but understanding born from years of observing how her illness shaped her relationships—how she could be sharp-tongued and critical with me because she knew I would not abandon her, and how she saved her worst behavior for the person she trusted most completely.

Dr. Del Cruz confirmed what I had long intuited through years of being her primary caretaker: "She acts this way with you because she knows you'll take care of her. She's not so sure about Wesley or Wendell, but she knows you'll handle things." This knowledge did not make her criticism easier to bear, but it gave me the context to see that her harshness was not rejection but a twisted form of trust—her way of testing whether I would remain constant even when she made constancy as difficult as possible.

Once Wesley had tried to take care of her for a month, his call came exactly as I had expected: "Come get her. I can't handle this." My mother's mental illness did not manifest as depression or withdrawal but as full-blown mania. Like the day she went grocery shopping, rear-ended someone's van, and then continued shopping as though nothing had happened—coming home with a smashed car and an attitude that dared anyone to question her. She responded to concern with anger, because anger was easier than explaining what it felt like to lose control of your own mind.

"I bet my grandmother had a hard time when Mama was young," I said to Dr. Del Cruz during one of our sessions, finally understanding that bipolar disorder does not suddenly appear in middle age but represents a lifetime of episodes earlier generations had no names for—beyond the knowledge that some people had storms in their minds that made them dangerous to themselves and others. When he agreed—"You're right, Janet"—I heard my grandmother's voice across the years saying, "Don't let her use you until she uses you up," advice that had seemed harsh when I was younger but now revealed itself as protection, wisdom from someone who had already learned the cost of loving someone whose illness could consume everyone around them if boundaries were not maintained.

Being my mother's caretaker was not just the practical burden of managing appointments and medications and crisis interventions, but the emotional burden of remaining loving in the face of behavior that quite obviously pushed love away—of accepting responsibility for someone who would criticize my every decision while depending on me to make those decisions correctly. "You're too damn smart," she would tell me. "Been smart ever since you started walking." And I would laugh and agree, because there was no point in arguing with someone whose illness made arguments pointless.

This was my education in the particular weight that falls on Black women in families—the expectation that we will be strong enough to handle whatever needs handling, wise enough to make decisions others cannot make, and resilient enough to absorb criticism and blame and keep functioning anyway. But it also became my education in understanding that this weight, heavy as it was, came with privileges that not everyone received—the privilege of being trusted with someone's most vulnerable moments, of being the person they turned to when everything else failed, of being loved enough to be hated when hate was the only emotion their illness allowed them to express safely.

There was also the matter of tradition and superstition, particularly with my uncle Ransom. When my mother was at her lowest, he insisted on trying all sorts of voodoo rituals to "fix" her. One time, he went to D.C. to see a woman who supposedly had the answers. He returned with a ten-dollar bill cut in half, placing one half above her bedroom door and the other in some hidden spot. The minute he left, I taped those two halves back together and spent the ten dollars. "Mama, we've got ten dollars to spend," I told her. It's almost funny thinking about it now—the absurdity of it all—but at the time, it was just one more layer of chaos to navigate.

But family, for better or worse, is the cornerstone of who

we are. It shapes us, tests us, and sometimes weighs on us in ways we never expected. Family is messy, complicated, and sometimes downright maddening. But it's also beautiful. It's where we find our greatest challenges and our greatest joys. On April 2, 2001, my mother, Helen Louise Singleton—the woman who gave me my name and the color of her eyes, my sweet mother—spread her wings and flew west to meet her ancestors.

The morning she left, I walked into her room and found her curled on the floor like the child she had once been, her body returned to the fetal position that had marked her beginning, her face wearing a smile that seemed to illuminate the entire room with knowledge I could not yet possess. When the EMS technician asked what state she was in, I told him, "She's *leaving me.*" There was no medical terminology adequate for what I was witnessing, no clinical language that could capture the transformation taking place before my eyes.

I knelt beside her and said, "Mother, I'm here." A small bubble of blood appeared at her nose and gently burst, and I knew I was witnessing her final breath—her last gift to me. The assurance that she would not leave without saying goodbye. That even in dying she was teaching me something about how to hold love and loss in the same moment without being destroyed by either. The EMS technician confirmed what I already knew; I had felt her departure like a change in atmospheric pressure, like the moment when day becomes evening and everything shifts into a different quality of light.

The peace that filled me as I looked at her smiling face was not the peace of resignation but the peace of completion—the understanding that she had lived fully and died ready, that whatever pain had marked her final days had been transformed in her final moments into something approaching joy. Mrs. Owens, my neighbor—whom I called my mature senior girlfriend—gave me the gift that would sustain me through the grief that followed when she told me that Mother had confided in her that the best time of her life was the time she spent with me. Not just the first three years when I lived with her full-time, but all the weekends afterward.

This revelation illuminated something I had not fully understood about the architecture of our relationship: that while I thought I was simply the beneficiary of her care, I had actually been the source of her greatest happiness. That in receiving her love, I had been giving her purpose. And in allowing her to shape me, I had been allowing her to complete herself—giving her the opportunity to pass on the particular wisdom that moves from Black mothers to Black daughters, a torch in a relay race that spans generations.

The following year—2002—just a month before Mother's one-year memorial, my brother Wesley surrendered his long fight with pancreatic cancer. He carried with him a piece of me that no one in the world would ever understand, no matter how much they tried. Ours was a bond forged by the water of the womb. In his final days, he had given me his power of attorney, saying that although he loved his wife, Wendy, dearly, he was concerned about recklessness when it came to spending.

And Aunt Polly Jones—she lived with that same grace and dignity I had known since I was three, serving the church and her community dutifully until she earned her wings on December 26, 2003, at the age of one hundred and one. Aunt Polly's passing meant that I had suffered the loss of loved ones three years in a row. I had barely the time to mourn each one fully, for death had kept its shadow cast across my skies. Mourning became dawn.

But a squirrel knows something we often forget. It gathers nuts in summer because winter will come. The squirrel understands that survival depends on preparation—on the work done when times are good. We humans must learn this same truth about friendship. The people who will stand with you in trying times and in your later years are the ones you chose to love and tend to when you were young.

When Glenn planned my 70th birthday in San Francisco, I watched this truth unfold before my eyes. Every single person he invited came. Most no longer lived in Baltimore. My dearest friend Gloria and her husband had moved to Sacramento back in 1988, but we never let distance silence our voices. Amber rode the train all the way across the country just to celebrate with me. The room was filled with

California friends too—people I had come to know since Glenn moved westward. We danced and laughed until our sides ached. These are the ones who become family, forged by covenant to stand in the gap left by the water of the womb.

I have always been careful about friendship. I do not give my trust quickly or easily. But when I do choose someone—when I decide they deserve a place in my heart—they stay there. Even now, I still have two girlfriends from my childhood neighborhood. Time and miles have stretched between us, but we still reach out to each other now and then.

Through all these years, I also kept close to my classmates from Garrison and Eastern High. Once a month, we would gather for lunch, sharing stories that grew sweeter with each telling. Then Covid-19 came and stole nearly two years from us. Some of my friends did not make it through. The last time we met before the pandemic, they spoke about how their bodies had begun to betray them at seventy. I told them, "That has not happened to me yet."

But when they saw me with my walker in the fall of 2024, their faces changed.

"Wait," they said, "what is going on?"

None of them knew—not even Amber. She walked straight to me and said, "How long have you been using this walker? Why didn't you tell me? If you needed help, I would have been there."

I told her, "Glenn comes every weekend, so why would I

trouble you? I remember you all talking about how everything falls apart at seventy. Well, I went to sleep one night at seventy-eight and woke up at seventy-nine, and something had shifted. That's when this started. It crept up on me slow and quiet. I don't know how I would have handled it if it had hit me all at once."

I have always been the organizer of our group, the one who found the best restaurants whenever we met. So when I mentioned the young man from Ghana who sometimes cooks for me, they lit up. "When are you inviting us for dinner?" they asked.

I laughed and shook my head. "Never. The next invitation you'll get is for my eightieth birthday." I looked at each of their faces. "When you get home today, mark February 1, 2025, on your calendar. Don't make any other plans for that day. Your invitation will come."

Later, Glenn asked what I wanted for my eightieth birthday. "A party!" I said without hesitation. When he asked where, I told him, "I grew up in Baltimore, and my classmates are here. It's time for me to have one back home."

My life has been gentle when it comes to love and friendship. I think younger people today struggle more with this than we did. At this age, romantic love for me mostly means having someone to sit with—someone whose presence makes the quiet hours less quiet.

The squirrel knows that winter comes for everyone. But if

you gather your people with the same care that the squirrel gathers its nuts, you will not face the cold alone.

At eighty, I am what my grandmother would have called a diamond of the sun—forged under pressures that have crushed other stones, polished by decades of friction against this land of my birth.

With my mother, Helen Singleton

8
SEASONS AND LESSONS

Life doesn't come with a manual, only seasons. Some bring sunshine, others bring storms, but each carries its own lesson. As I look back, I see how the shifting seasons of my life—moments of joy, sorrow, struggle, and triumph—were all classrooms for wisdom. Growth doesn't always feel good, but it always leaves something behind: perspective.

This chapter reflects on what life has taught me, not in the silence of reflection alone, but in the noise, the ache, the laughter, and the letting go.

* * *

NO REGRETS

Freedom flows from living without regrets—a wisdom only life can teach. In eighty years, I have seen and done things that others might spend a lifetime wondering about or wishing they had experienced. I lived by one rule: *No regrets.* This did not mean I never made mistakes or endured difficult days; it meant I chose to stand by every decision, learn from every stumble, and keep moving forward.

To live without regrets is to understand that life comes without rehearsal. Moments define us. Small choices become markers in time. People shape our paths in ways we could never foresee. I learned early that things would not always unfold as planned, and even the purest intentions could birth unintended consequences. Rather than allowing those moments to weigh me down, I received them with grace. "You will encounter bumps in the road," I would whisper to my soul, "but this is simply life." Regret is a shackle. It keeps you stuck in the past, unable to fully embrace the present or imagine the future.

My approach became one of humble surrender, a courage that carried me through every season. From the dreams and uncertainties of my youth to the wisdom and clarity of later years, I trusted my choices. This does not mean I always chose correctly—no one does. But I believed deeply that every experience, even the most difficult, carried lessons within its folds. When I became pregnant with Glenn and realized I would raise him as a single mother, when I chose to keep him rather than give him up for adoption—these were weighty decisions. Life shapes you in ways the mind cannot anticipate, and every moment has been worthwhile.

I have lived a full life. I have made choices. I have made mistakes. Do I carry regrets? No. I have contemplated this truth at every phase, because life does move in phases. You are not born and then remain unchanged until death. At each stage, no regrets have taken root in my heart. Life has been generous with me.

When I look backward, I do not dwell on possibilities that never bloomed, actions I did not take, or opportunities that passed me by. Instead, I gaze back with gratitude, because my life now holds beauty, and every single decision I have ever made has delivered me to this precise moment. I told Glenn once that we have experienced, as a family and as individuals, bumps in the road. But this is life's way. It will become difficult. It will be muddy and rough. You will feel weary and confused. Sometimes despair will visit your door. But eventually, everything finds its proper place, and you discover clarity and reason to continue.

One of my deepest offerings to anyone walking this earth is this: live boldly, embrace the rises and falls, and do not waste precious time questioning yourself after choices are made. These were the very words I shared with everyone at my eightieth birthday celebration. To live with regrets is to deny the beauty of who you are in this moment, molded by every decision and every breath. I urge you to live openly, with courage flowing through your veins, so that one day you might look back and declare with a peaceful heart: *No regrets.*

The soul knows its own path. Trust it. Walk it. Love it. For in the end, regret is simply love afraid to dance with what has already been written in the stars.

> Regret is a shackle, it keeps you stuck in the past, unable to fully embrace the present or imagine the future."

— JANET PERKINS

DO NOT OVER-PLAN

Life presents itself as a curious blend of unpredictability and divine order, chaos dancing with control in eternal rhythm. We dwell in a world where planning receives praise as the cornerstone of success. Schedules, agendas, and meticulously crafted goals dominate the modern story of purposeful living. But what unfolds when life refuses to follow our careful designs? For me, the answer rests in embracing the unpredictable, the spontaneous, and the beautifully chaotic moments that render life sacred and worth living.

Planning holds its own merit—I acknowledge this. It provides structure to our deepest longings and helps us traverse the densities of earthly existence. But for souls like mine, the true art of living dwells in finding balance between preparation and the willingness to flow with life's divine surprises. No amount of planning can prepare the heart for the unexpected turns that define our sacred journey. Life, as I have come to understand, is meant to be lived in the present moment, with space for spontaneity and wonder to enter. People burden themselves with excessive planning, yet life unfolds according to its own divine timing.

One of the most persistent illusions about planning is that it grants us dominion over our lives. The truth whispers differently: life flows according to laws beyond our comprehension. You may plan every detail of your day, week, or year, but a single unexpected event—an illness, a loss, or even a chance encounter—can transform those plans completely. I did not, even in my wildest dreams, plan to conceive at eighteen. Yet this became my reality—and my greatest teacher.

I have observed friends and family carefully mapping every aspect of their existence, only to discover disappointment when reality failed to match their expectations. In my later years, I watched my son live in a manner directly opposite to mine. He scheduled everything on his calendar, even phone calls with loved ones. On certain days, I witnessed his distress when events refused to follow his predetermined path. My heart ached for him, seeing how such attachments disturbed his peace for hours afterward. I have also watched countless souls become so consumed with their plans that they forget to inhabit the present moment. They spend precious energy plotting futures while missing the miracles unfolding before them. The irony is clear: while planning creates an illusion of preparedness, it can blind us to opportunities that do not fit our narrow expectations.

Life, as I have learned through living, is too vast and too mysterious for rigid structures. I keep a small scrapbook—begun in my youth—where I recorded dreams of who I might become, things I wanted to do, and places I longed to visit. Yet I always understood that circumstances could shift, and I trusted my capacity to meet whatever arrived at my door. You must leave space for life to surprise you, because it will—whether or not you feel ready.

A delicate boundary exists between planning and excessive planning. Planning means creating a framework, a gentle guide toward desired destinations. Excessive planning attempts to control every detail, leaving no room for flexibility or divine intervention. Excessive planning becomes a prison. It breeds frustration when reality refuses to conform, and it prevents us from adapting to new circumstances. Life does not flow in straight lines; it moves like a river, with currents and eddies, with unexpected turns toward destinations we could never imagine.

My approach to life involved trusting myself and the natural rhythm of existence. I believed that too many rigid plans created limitations, causing us to miss the wonderful, unexpected gifts life offers continuously. While I honored goals and aspirations, I also knew that often the most precious experiences arose from flowing with the moment. Many of my most treasured memories were never planned. They emerged from saying "yes" to spontaneous journeys, engaging strangers in meaningful conversation, or simply walking without a predetermined destination. I hope you can understand this wisdom—that true strength lives in adaptability, in moving gracefully with life's changes while knowing you possess the capacity to meet whatever comes next.

Living without excessive planning does not mean living

without purpose. It means setting intentions and priorities while remaining receptive to change. It means knowing your desires without becoming so attached to outcomes that you miss other divine opportunities.

For me, this balance has unlocked a fulfilling existence. I establish broad intentions for my path—career aspirations, personal growth, meaningful connections—but I leave space for life to surprise me. More often than not, those surprises surpass anything my limited mind could have conceived.

Uncertainty often appears as a source of anxiety, yet it can also become a gateway to freedom. When you stop trying to control every aspect of your existence, you open yourself to infinite possibilities. You become more adaptable, more resilient, and more attuned to the eternal present moment.

Consider this: how often does fear of the unknown prevent us from embracing risks or exploring new territories? When you learn to welcome uncertainty, you discover that the unknown is fertile ground for growth. Within mystery, we uncover new passions, create meaningful bonds, and find the strength to withstand all challenges.

Releasing the need to control everything becomes a form of liberation. It allows you to focus on what truly matters: the souls you love, the experiences that bring joy, and the lessons that shape your sacred path.

When you surrender control, you also stop comparing yourself to others. You cease measuring your progress against another's timeline and begin appreciating your own unique unfolding. This shift in perception is incredibly liberating—one of the greatest gifts you can offer yourself.

Life reveals itself as a journey, not a checklist to complete. It manifests as a series of moments, both planned and unplanned, weaving together to create a story that belongs only to you. My counsel flows simply: receive life as it comes. Set your intentions, know your heart's desires, but allow existence to have its say. You may find yourself walking a path you never envisioned, yet one richer and more fulfilling than anything your mind could have designed.

In my eyes, this is the true beauty of being alive—the eternal dance between our will and the Divine's infinite wisdom, between our plans and life's mysterious grace.

You've got to leave room for life to surprise you, because it will, whether you're ready or not.

— JANET PERKINS

YOU HAVE TO ACT

Faith is a powerful force, a foundation of hope that sustains the soul. It encourages us to trust in something greater than ourselves, guiding us through trials and uncertainties. Yet faith alone, without action, resembles planting seeds without watering them, hoping they will bloom. Life demands more than passive observation; it requires active participation, intentional decisions, and consistent effort from those who truly wish to live.

Faith holds beauty and necessity—this I honor deeply. Sometimes we must allow life to unfold according to its own divine timing. However, you cannot simply sit back, offer prayers, and wait for gifts to arrive at your door. Faith must join hands with effort, for life presents itself as a series of choices, and every choice demands action, even if it is only the first small step forward. You must act. You cannot remain seated in prayer, expecting abundance to be delivered without your participation. Life calls for decisions, and each decision requires movement, however modest it may be.

Faith provides direction; effort becomes the force that propels you onward. Consider standing at the base of a mountain you wish to climb. Faith tells you the summit awaits your arrival, but only effort moves your feet along the ascending path. Without action, your vision of reaching the peak remains forever a dream dwelling only in your heart.

Many people fall into the trap of waiting for the "perfect

moment" or relying solely on divine intervention to transform their circumstances. While believing in the possibilities that faith offers is vital, recognizing the role of personal responsibility is equally important. Life requires a sacred partnership between belief and deed.

Throughout my years, I have observed people waiting and hoping, dreaming without doing. But my understanding flowed differently. From my youth, I grasped that the only way to achieve dreams was to act upon them. I was never one to sit idly by, expecting circumstances to arrange themselves favorably. Even when uncertainty or fear arose, I pushed myself to take that necessary step. If you want something, don't just think about it—go get it.

Every moment of existence presents us with choices, whether small or momentous. Choosing to rise each morning, deciding to pursue a calling, or making time for relationships—these represent acts of faith and action unified. Understanding that even indecision is a choice proves crucial. When we fail to act, we still decide—to remain static. By taking the first step, regardless of its size, we demonstrate our willingness to work in harmony with our faith.

I understand that fear sometimes restrains us and that the unknown can feel overwhelming. Yet I also know that everything worthwhile requires courage—a willingness to embrace risk and accept mistakes along the journey. When I left my husband, I possessed no certainty about my path.

The decision to make a down payment on a house emerged spontaneously, yet I knew I wanted a different life than the one I inhabited at that moment. My existence stands as proof that action, however modest, creates momentum. I want others to experience the excitement of possibility, of taking charge of their destiny.

Throughout history, people have achieved greatness by uniting faith with effort. From inventors and activists to ordinary individuals pursuing extraordinary dreams, the common thread binding their stories is their willingness to act upon their beliefs. Many social movements, including the struggle for civil rights, were built upon faith in a better tomorrow and driven by tireless action. Activists prayed for transformation, yet they also marched, protested, and advocated for justice. Do not wait for permission or the "right" time, for perfect timing never arrives. Act with purpose, move forward with determination. In the end, remember that possessing dreams alone is insufficient; you must labor to manifest them in the world. And taking action once does not suffice—consistency becomes the key to achieving meaningful results. Faith is not a single declaration, and action is not a solitary effort. Both require persistence and unwavering commitment.

Consistency builds momentum. It transforms small efforts into significant outcomes over time. Just as a river carves through stone not by force but by persistence, consistent action can overcome obstacles that appear immovable.

Do not merely pray for change—labor for it. Do not simply hope for success—pursue it with your whole being. Unite your faith with action, and you will discover that life rewards those who dare to step into the unknown with trust and determination.

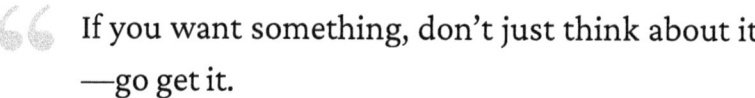 If you want something, don't just think about it —go get it.

— JANET PERKINS

GUARD YOUR INTEGRITY

If one trait existed above all others that I valued, it was integrity. To me, integrity flows beyond mere honesty—it means being true to yourself, standing by your values, and doing what is right *for you*, even when difficulty surrounds you. Integrity is often defined as adherence to moral and ethical principles, but I believe it reaches deeper than that. It does not merely concern following rules or societal expectations; it involves aligning your actions with your inner values. Integrity means maintaining consistency of character, regardless of the situation. It calls for standing firm when adversity confronts you and making choices that resonate with your sense of right and wrong.

This understanding of integrity illuminates its inherently personal nature. What proves right for one soul might not align with another's beliefs, yet both can act with integrity if their decisions remain true to their own values.

I have observed, through countless seasons, how easily people can be swayed by circumstances or influenced by others. But for me, integrity remained nonnegotiable. During my years of service at the Social Security Administration, it mattered not what occurred around me—I performed my work to the best of my ability regardless of who was watching or whether acknowledgment ever came my way.

The modern world overflows with distractions, temptations, and pressures that test a person's integrity. Social media, peer pressure, and the constant flood of external opinions make it easier than ever to stray from one's core beliefs.

I have witnessed people compromise their values for acceptance, success, or convenience. This is understandable—life often presents moments where taking the easier path feels appealing. Standing by your truth does not always bring comfort, and it can sometimes feel isolating. However, choosing integrity sets individuals apart and builds a life of authenticity and respect.

Your integrity belongs to you and to no one else. To live a fulfilling existence, you must know who you are and remain grounded in that knowledge. Integrity does not mean perfection; it means staying aligned with your own values and principles, even when the world around you attempts to pull you in different directions.

Integrity manifests in the choices we make each day. It appears in small decisions—like owning up to a mistake at work—and in large ones, like walking away from a toxic relationship or refusing to compromise your values for financial gain.

For me, one of the most powerful examples of integrity comes from standing up for myself in situations where remaining silent would have been easier. Life will always test you, and I knew that truth well. I faced moments where doing the easy thing felt tempting, but I always chose to stick to what I believed in. That choice has always brought me peace and a deeper sense of fulfillment. In my understanding, it is better to lose an opportunity or face a setback than to compromise on integrity. At the end of the day, you have only yourself to answer to.

Many people confuse integrity with honesty, but they are not the same. Honesty is a component of integrity, but it does not represent the complete picture. Honesty concerns truth-telling, while integrity involves truth-living.

For example, you can be honest and still lack integrity if your actions do not align with your values. Integrity is the consistency between what you say, believe, and do. It represents a state of being rather than merely a momentary act. Compromising your integrity may provide temporary relief or success, but it often comes at a cost. When you act against your values, you create internal conflict that can lead to regret, self-doubt, and a loss of self-respect.

I have seen people succeed in the short term by compromising their integrity, but their victories felt hollow. Over time, those compromises eroded their sense of self, leaving them feeling disconnected and unfulfilled. True success is measured not by external achievements but by the alignment between your actions and your values.

Integrity is crucial not only in your relationship with yourself but also in your relationships with others. It builds trust, respect, and authenticity. When you live with integrity, people know they can rely on you, and your connections become deeper and more meaningful.

Yet living with integrity can sometimes strain relationships. People may not always understand or agree with your choices, and standing by your truth can create conflict. But I believe any relationship worth having will respect your integrity and support your need to be true to yourself.

In professional settings, integrity often serves as the cornerstone of success and respect. It means delivering on your promises, being accountable for your actions, and maintaining ethical standards even when no one is watching.

Throughout my career, I faced moments when my integrity was tested. Whether dealing with ethical dilemmas or workplace politics, I found that standing by my values was always the right choice. While this path was not always the easiest, it earned me the respect and trust of colleagues, clients, and mentors.

One of the most important legacies we can leave is instilling integrity in the next generation. Whether through parenting, mentorship, or simply setting an example, we hold the power to inspire others to live authentically.

Teaching integrity is not about preaching; it is about demonstrating. It means showing young people that doing the right thing is not always easy, but it is always worthwhile. When children see adults standing by their values, they learn to do the same. I see that in my son, Glenn, and it fills me with pride. A leader with integrity does not merely talk about values—they live them. They make tough decisions, hold themselves accountable, and prioritize fairness and transparency.

These qualities not only benefit the organizations they serve but also leave a lasting impact on the people they lead.

Find your own inner compass and trust it completely. Integrity, I believe, concerns not only how others see you but also how you see yourself. Live in a way that makes you proud of who you are, no matter the situation. Hold on to that integrity with all your strength, because when everything else fades away, it remains the one thing you can truly count on.

The soul that lives with integrity walks in harmony with the divine order of existence, creating ripples of truth that touch every life it encounters. In this sacred alignment of inner truth with outer action, we discover not just who we are but who we are meant to become.

Integrity isn't about being perfect; it is about staying aligned with your own values and principles, even when the world around you tries to pull you in different directions.

— JANET PERKINS

LISTEN MORE, TALK LESS

These days, it seems everyone is speaking. It doesn't help that nearly everyone can now afford a podcast microphone. Yet with all this talking, no one is truly listening, and we wonder why so much misunderstanding fills our world today. When I find myself among young people, it often feels as though no one receives the words being offered. They talk constantly, filling every silence with chatter, convinced they have all the answers or eager to prove something. Being in their presence can feel burdensome—everyone speaks, yet no one truly hears. If one truth has revealed itself to me over the years, it is this: wisdom flows not only from speaking but more often from listening. Some of the most valuable moments in life come not from talking, but from remaining quiet and receiving what others have to share.

When I was younger, I did not fully understand this lesson. I believed that if something occupied my mind, it required immediate expression. But as the seasons passed, life taught me the value of stepping back, of absorbing what others had experienced and learned. I discovered that by speaking less, I opened myself to perspectives and insights I might have otherwise missed. Listening involves more than simply waiting for your turn to speak. True listening means setting aside ego, preconceived notions, and the urge to interrupt—it requires seeking to understand another's heart and seeing life from their point of view.

When I was raising Glenn, I learned that sometimes all he needed was a listening ear—not a lecture, not advice. With friends and loved ones too, I found that simply being present without speaking often spoke more powerfully than any words could. I began asking myself, *"What can I discover here?"* And it amazed me how much you uncover when you remain patient enough to truly listen.

You cannot listen if you are always speaking. As we used to say, *"We can sing together, but we cannot talk together at the same time."* So many people make life harder than it needs to be by refusing to pause and actually hear what is being offered. Hearing is passive—it is merely the physical act of perceiving sound. Listening, by contrast, is active and intentional. It means processing, interpreting, and seeking to understand the meaning within what is being shared.

I have come to realize that listening is a skill, one that requires practice. It is not enough to nod your head or say, *"I understand."* True listening involves asking thoughtful questions to clarify or deepen understanding, maintaining eye contact, and using body language to show engagement. It means reflecting back what you have heard to confirm comprehension. These small actions can transform any conversation, making another person feel valued and truly heard.

Silence is often misunderstood as awkward or empty, yet it is a powerful tool in communication. Silence gives people space to process their thoughts, reflect on what has been said, and feel safe enough to share more deeply. I have found that embracing silence in conversations often leads to richer and more meaningful exchanges. When you resist the urge to fill every pause, you allow the other person the space to fully express themselves.

Over time, I have also realized that listening helps you miss nothing of life's essence. Too often we focus so intently on what we want to say next that we miss the beauty unfolding around us. Listening is the foundation of healthy relationships, whether personal or professional. To listen is to demonstrate respect, to build trust, and to cultivate understanding.

In romantic relationships, listening allows partners to feel seen and valued. It prevents misunderstandings and strengthens emotional connection. In friendships, it creates sacred space for vulnerability. And in professional settings, it leads to stronger teamwork, innovation, and problem-solving. I have lived through moments where failing to listen caused misunderstandings or missed opportunities, and I have also experienced times when choosing to listen profoundly shaped my life.

I remember one instance when a friend came to me with a problem. My first instinct was to offer solutions, but instead I chose simply to listen. By the end of our conversation, they thanked me—not for fixing their issue, but for being present and allowing them to speak. That moment taught me that people often do not need answers; they need to be heard. When you commit to listening, people open themselves in ways they never would if you were talking over them. And in those moments, you discover your own soul expanding.

Empathy forms the heart of true listening. It involves placing yourself in another person's position and seeing the world through their eyes. Empathy allows you to connect on deeper levels and respond with understanding rather than judgment. Listening with empathy can transform conflicts into opportunities for growth. It helps calm tensions, repair relationships, and create a sense of unity.

In today's digital world, communication often occurs through screens. While technology offers benefits, it can also make genuine listening more challenging. Text messages, emails, and social media lack the subtleties of face-to-face interactions. To truly listen in a digital age, we must be intentional about how we engage. This might mean setting aside time for phone calls or in-person meetings, reading messages carefully before responding, or being mindful of tone and context.

Listening more than you speak—that is where learning occurs. You do not need to do things exactly like someone else, but everyone possesses something to teach. I never dismiss people, because we have all experienced life, and you never know who might hold the answer you need. If one truth has revealed itself to me, it is that our world right now needs more listeners.

> Listening isn't just about waiting for your turn to speak; it's about understanding someone else's heart, really seeing things from their point of view.

— JANET PERKINS

SAY WHAT YOU MEAN & MEAN WHAT YOU MEAN

One thing I've come to hold dear is the power of my word. I was raised to believe that when you say something, you should mean it, and when you mean it, you should follow through. Words are precious; they have weight and meaning, and they can either build or break trust. I've learned that by saying what I mean and meaning what I say, I've been able to build a life filled with respect and genuine relationships.

I can remember times when people said one thing and did another, and how hurtful that was. So I promised myself that if I made a commitment or gave my word, I'd do my best to keep it. I'd rather say nothing at all than say something I don't intend to stand behind. If I tell you I'll be there, you can count on it. If I give you advice, you know it's from the heart. There's strength in that, and it builds the kind of trust that's rare these days.

Keeping your word isn't just about being reliable; it's about showing respect—for others and for yourself. When you make a promise, you create an expectation. Breaking that promise erodes trust, while keeping it reinforces your integrity. Over time, I've learned that people judge you not by your intentions but by your actions—and your actions begin with your words.

Sometimes speaking your truth isn't easy. I've had tough conversations and made difficult choices, but I've found that facing things head-on and saying what I truly feel has always paid off. People know where they stand with me, and there's peace in that. There's no second-guessing or wondering. I don't have to keep track of what I said because it always comes from a place of honesty.

This lesson isn't just about being truthful with others—it's about being honest with yourself, too. When you can look in the mirror and know that your words and actions line up, you walk a little taller. You feel at peace. And that's something I wish for everyone.

Words are not just a reflection of our intentions; they also carry emotional weight. I've come to appreciate how my words can impact someone's mood, self-esteem, or outlook on life. Compliments, encouragement, and expressions of gratitude have the power to uplift, while criticism or indifference can wound deeply.

There have been moments when a simple "I believe in you" made all the difference to someone struggling with doubt. Conversely, I've learned to avoid speaking in anger or frustration, as those words often cause unnecessary harm.

In relationships, words are the glue that holds everything together. Trust, love, and understanding all hinge on honest and open communication. I've found that when I am clear about my feelings, intentions, and expectations, my relationships flourish.

For instance, expressing gratitude and appreciation strengthens bonds, while addressing conflicts with honesty prevents misunderstandings from festering. The more I've focused on saying what I mean and meaning what I say, the more my relationships have become grounded in mutual respect and authenticity.

There have also been times when keeping my word was challenging. Life throws curveballs, and circumstances change, making it difficult to follow through on commitments. In these situations, I've learned that honesty is the best approach. Communicating openly about the challenges I'm facing and renegotiating my commitments has allowed me to maintain trust, even in difficult times.

Another challenge is dealing with people who don't value their own word. It's disheartening to invest in relationships or collaborations where others fail to follow through. However, these experiences have reinforced my commitment to staying true to my values, regardless of how others behave.

Words and actions are two sides of the same coin. Saying what you mean is important, but following through with actions is what gives your words meaning. I've learned that actions often speak louder than words, but the combination of the two is what truly builds trust and respect.

When people see that your actions align with your words, they know they can count on you. This alignment creates a sense of reliability and authenticity that is invaluable in both personal and professional relationships. Keeping my word has also been a cornerstone of my personal growth. It has taught me discipline, self-awareness, and accountability. When I commit to something—whether it's a personal goal or a promise to someone else—I view it as an opportunity to grow and strengthen my character.

So say what you mean, and mean what you say. It's a simple lesson, but one that's brought me a lot of freedom and respect over the years.

Keeping your word isn't just about being reliable; it's about showing respect for others and yourself.

— JANET PERKINS

SANKOFA: REACH BACK

I'll never forget my first visit to Ghana in 2004. It was one of those trips that stays with you forever. I remember walking through a market in Accra, surrounded by colors and life. It was there that I first came across the Adinkra symbol of Sankofa.

I didn't know what it meant at first. It was a beautiful symbol—shaped like a heart with a curl at the top, or sometimes like a bird reaching back to pluck something, like an egg, from its own tail. I was fascinated by it, as though it was calling to me. When I asked one of the locals about it, they explained that Sankofa means "go back and fetch it." It's a reminder that no matter how far you've come in life, it's important to look back, to learn from the past, and to bring forward the lessons that guide you.

That message touched me deeply. I saw my own life in the meaning of Sankofa. I've always believed in moving forward, but standing there in Accra, surrounded by the history and culture of my forebears, it hit me in a different way. I thought about my ancestors, the sacrifices they made, and the spirit they carried that allowed me to stand where I am today. How could I not reach back when so many had done it for me? How could I not honor the struggles and triumphs of those before me by moving forward?

The Sankofa symbol reminds us that our past isn't something to be forgotten. It's a well of wisdom, a guide, a reminder of where we started and how far we've come. But it also speaks to the future—that we have a duty to extend a hand to others, to make their paths a little easier, just as someone once did for us.

During that visit to Ghana, I saw Sankofa everywhere—on fabrics, carvings, and even painted on the walls of schools. It was more than a cultural emblem; it was a way of life. It felt as though the people there carried this truth in their hearts, weaving it into their communities and their relationships.

Now I carry a silver medallion of Sankofa myself, a gift from Glenn as part of his 2022 Homecoming—an initiative he started in 2019 to help African-Americans find their way back to the land of their ancestors. It's no surprise he named the initiative *Sankofa Homecoming*.

I've tried to embody that spirit in my own life. One of the most beautiful parts of growing older is realizing the importance of reaching back. I believe that if you're fortunate enough to find success or happiness, you have a responsibility to help those coming up behind you. Life isn't meant to be a one-person journey, where you leave everyone else behind. No, I believe in making sure the people coming along have an easier path than I did.

I've had wonderful people who reached back to me when I needed a little push or a helping hand. Whether it was family, friends, or even strangers, I was lifted by their kindness. And that's something I've always wanted to pass along.

Reaching back can be as simple as sharing advice, lending a hand, or just being a source of encouragement. It doesn't always require much, but it can mean everything to the person receiving it.

Reaching back is a way to honor those who helped you along the way. It's about showing gratitude by giving of yourself. I've been blessed in many ways, and I can't imagine not wanting to share that with others. I hope that every young person who finds success will feel the same—that they'll remember to reach back. Because when we lift each other up, we all grow stronger. This, to me, is one of life's greatest responsibilities.

So now, when I think of Sankofa, I think of Ghana, yes, but also of the countless people in my life who have helped me fetch the pieces I needed to keep moving forward. And I think of the joy I've found in doing the same for others.

> Reaching back is a way to honor those who helped you along the way. It's about showing gratitude by giving of yourself.
>
> — JANET PERKINS

BE WILLING TO MAKE SACRIFICES

Every now and then, I think of the biggest decision of my life: having a child at eighteen. Choosing to keep my baby—rather than putting him up for adoption as Daddy had suggested—was the greatest sacrifice I ever made. The day I decided to keep him, I sacrificed my teen years. I put the possibility of attaining my educational goals on the line. I gave up my freedom to enjoy life as a single woman in order to take on a lifetime of motherhood, at the time as a single mother. If there's one thing I've come to understand, it's that sacrifices are part of any worthwhile journey. There's no shortcut to success, happiness, or a fulfilling life. If you want something meaningful, you have to be willing to give something up to get it. It's a hard truth, but it's one I've lived by.

Throughout my life, I've had to make sacrifices, and each one has taught me the value of what I was working toward. Sometimes it meant sacrificing my time, sometimes my comfort, but it was always worth it. When I was raising my child, I had to put his needs ahead of my own countless times. I gave up nights out, opportunities, and even sleep, but I knew the love and care I poured into him was worth more than anything else.

Sacrifice doesn't mean you're giving up on your dreams. Quite the opposite—it means you're investing in something bigger. Sometimes you have to put aside immediate gratification to achieve something lasting. I think of sacrifices as seeds you plant, knowing they'll grow into something beautiful one day. You might not see the results right away, but trust me, they'll come.

Now I look back on my journey and think of how much impact that one single decision has had on the world—how many lives have been touched by this child of mine, how his work has shaped the way race and equity are approached across various sectors globally, and how many people have been able to make a living through his vision.

So, I tell people to be ready for the hard work—for giving up small comforts in service of big dreams. Be ready to make sacrifices, but also take pride in them, because they are what shape your life and make the journey worthwhile. In the end, you'll see that what you gave up was small compared to the joy and fulfillment that comes from achieving something truly meaningful. And that, to me, is what life is all about. Because if you want to leave the world better than you found it, you're going to have to give something of yourself.

We're all just here for a while, passing through. The world keeps spinning, and when we're gone, it's those coming after us who will push it forward in whatever way they see fit. That part doesn't worry me. What I focus on is the now—my present. What do I want to do while I'm here? What can I contribute to help them build their future?

Once I'm gone, I'll be gone. And the best thing I can hope for is that they'll have memories—memories of things I said, things I did. Some of it will be useful, some of it won't matter much. But that's life, isn't it? In a nutshell, it's about doing what you can, when you can, and trusting that it will have an impact, big or small.

I've heard people say how messy, tangled, and confusing life is, but I don't see it that way. Sure, I've had challenges—who hasn't? But I've found that the key is to keep moving. If I've got a problem, I pray on it and ask for the Lord's help, but I don't just sit there. I get up and do something about it.

I've been fortunate to have people around me who embody that same energy. I've seen folks take the bull by the horns, determined to face whatever comes their way. They don't get stuck. If something doesn't work, they try another way. If it does, they build on it. That's the spirit I've always admired—the willingness to act, adapt, and keep pushing forward.

Sacrifice is at the heart of all that. You have to be willing to give of yourself, knowing that the outcome isn't always guaranteed. It's not easy, but it's necessary. It's not about avoiding challenges—it's about meeting them head-on, with faith, determination, and the courage to keep going.

Sacrifice doesn't mean you're giving up on your dreams. Quite the opposite—it means you're investing in bigger.

— JANET PERKINS

BE A PARENT

Trust me on this one. I know that being a parent today is one of the most difficult things to do. I was fortunate to begin my parenting journey when things weren't quite this bad—when the economy wasn't so harsh, when families lived closer to one another, and when the "village" could more easily help raise a child.

Parenthood is not for the faint of heart. It's one of the most challenging jobs you'll ever take on, and yet it comes with no manual, no instruction booklet, and certainly no pay. But it is also the most important job you'll ever have. Raising a child means shaping a life, molding a future, and leaving a legacy. That's no small thing.

I've seen many young parents—some doing their best, some overwhelmed, and some not fully understanding what they signed up for. And I always want to tell them: if you've got children, be a parent. Not just a provider of food and shelter, not just someone who gives commands and expects obedience. Be present. Be engaged. Be the person your child can look up to, lean on, and learn from.

When I think about children, I always see them as wide-open books—blank canvases, fresh clay. They don't come into this world with baggage or preconceived notions; they arrive with possibilities. And as their parent, you're the artist, the potter. Every word you speak and every action you take shapes that child in ways you may not even realize.

That's why it is so important to approach parenting with care, patience, and love.

I've heard people say, "Children are hard to raise," and while I understand what they mean, I don't entirely agree. Children can be easy if you let them be. They don't need fancy things or grand gestures. What they need is love, attention, and guidance. They need to feel safe, valued, and heard. They need to know that, no matter what, you've got their back.

One thing I've noticed over the years is how often parents dismiss their children: "Go sit down. Don't touch that. Stop asking questions." It's as if they see their kids as little nuisances instead of little people. But if you don't acknowledge your children as individuals, you risk losing them before they've even had a chance to grow. I've always loved that quote by Kahlil Gibran about children—he said they are not really ours to keep; they're loaned to us. And that is so true. Our job is to guide them, to love them, and to prepare them for a life that belongs to them, not us. That takes wisdom—and a whole lot of listening.

One of the most challenging aspects of raising Glenn was his hyper-curiosity. He asked so many questions, never knowing—or minding—whether I was in the mood to answer or not. It took wisdom to navigate that part of him, which he still carries into adulthood. I made a point of listening to him—not just hearing his words, but truly listening to what he was trying to say. Whether it was a story about his day or a dream he had for the future, I wanted him to know his voice mattered. And let me tell you, that makes all the difference. When a child feels seen and heard, they blossom. They develop confidence. They learn to trust themselves—and to trust you.

Dreams. Every child has them. Some want to be doctors or teachers. Others want to be artists or musicians. And as parents, it's easy to want to steer them toward something "practical," something we think will guarantee their success. But that's not our job. Our job is to support them in what they want to do—not what we think they should do.

I remember when Glenn started his company at twenty-six. At first, I wasn't sure, but I had learned to trust his ability to make the right decisions for himself. Did I worry a bit? Of course I did. I knew what doing racial equity work in America entails—how pushing conversations about diversity and inclusion in schools and workplaces can easily make you an enemy in these United States. But then I saw the passion in his eyes, the way they lit up when he talked about the experiences he had gathered as an admissions officer at Penn, and I knew I couldn't stand in his way. So I gave him my blessing and wished him well. And you know what? He found his path. He turned that love for representation into something meaningful, and I couldn't be prouder.

Children will stumble—that's just part of growing up. They'll hit brick walls, make mistakes, and face challenges they don't yet know how to overcome. And when that happens, it's your job to guide them, not control them. Help them find their way around the wall, but don't push them through it on your terms.

I've seen too many parents try to micromanage their kids' lives, deciding every step for them—what they need, when they need it, and why they need it. More often than not, it backfires. Children who are overly controlled end up feeling stifled, resentful, or worse, lost. They grow up not knowing who they are because they were never allowed to figure it out for themselves.

As a parent, your role is to provide support and guidance—not to dictate. Let your children make choices, even if you don't agree with them. Let them learn from their mistakes. Trust that they have the strength and wisdom to find their own way, with you cheering them on from the sidelines.

Here's something often overlooked in parenting: self-love. If you don't love yourself, you can't fully love anyone else—not even your children. That's a hard truth, but it's one I've learned over the years. Parenting is demanding. It can drain you physically, emotionally, and mentally. If you're constantly giving without taking time to refill your own cup, you'll burn out. And when that happens, you're no good to anyone—not your children, not your partner, and certainly not yourself.

So take care of yourself. Nurture your own passions. Maintain your friendships. And don't be afraid to ask for help when you need it. Show your children what self-love looks like. Teach them that it's okay to prioritize their own well-being. Because when they see you loving yourself, they'll learn to love themselves too.

I remember an experience I had with Glenn's personal assistant in Ghana on one of my visits. You see, Jeho had this habit of avoiding going into restaurants with us. He always had some excuse or another. On this particular night, he planned to drop Glenn and me off at the restaurant and either go somewhere else or wait in the car. Glenn asked him, "Aren't you coming with us?"

Jeho hesitated, gave Glenn that "don't push it" kind of look, and said, "No, sir," with a grin on his face. I wasn't having it. "Yes, you are," I said—and there was no room for debate.

Now, let me be clear—Jeho could've said no to me, too. He's grown, after all. But there's something about respect, the kind you earn from the way you carry yourself and the things you say over the years. Jeho knew who I was—the elder of the bunch—and I guess that held influence for him. So he sighed, relented, and said, "Alright, Mom, I'll go."

As we made our way upstairs to the restaurant, got settled, and started looking through the menu, I leaned over to Jeho and said, "You know, Jeho, the children are watching you." He gave me this puzzled look, so I continued: "They've been watching you from the moment they could walk and talk. That starts at about two years old. From then on, they're studying you—what you do, how you speak, how you treat people, and how you carry yourself. They don't miss a thing. And that's why, from the time they're that small, you have to be careful. You have to live in a way you'd be proud for them to imitate."

Jeho nodded, but I could see he was really thinking about it. I wasn't trying to lecture him; I just wanted him to understand the responsibility we have as adults, especially when little ones are in the picture.

It's not about being perfect—Lord knows none of us are. But it's about being intentional—intentional with your actions, your words, and the way you treat others. Kids don't just hear what you say; they watch what you do. And you better believe they're taking notes.

I told Jeho, "You have to be confident in yourself, in the decisions you make, and in the way you live your life. That confidence? It shows. It teaches them to be confident too. And if you're inconsistent or unsure, they'll pick up on that as well."

That night, I could see a shift in Jeho. He wasn't just there for the food anymore; he was present, engaged. He even laughed and joked with Glenn and me in a way he hadn't in a long time.

Maybe it was just a small moment, but to me it was a reminder of how much influence we have, whether we realize it or not. We're role models from the moment those little eyes and ears start paying attention—and that's not a responsibility to take lightly.

Parenting isn't about perfection. It's about love, effort, and showing up every day, even when it's hard. It's about being there for your kids, cheering them on, and helping them become the best versions of themselves.

When I look at my child now—grown and thriving—I feel a huge sense of pride. Not just in what he has accomplished, but in the person he has become. He's kind, confident, and strong. And I like to think that's because I chose to be a parent in the truest sense of the word.

So to all the young parents out there, especially the single moms, hear me when I say this: You got this. Be a parent—not just in name, but in action. Love your children fiercely. Support their dreams. Guide them with patience and kindness. And most importantly, love yourself. Because when you do that, you'll be the kind of parent your children need—and deserve.

" Be a parent. Be present. Be engaged. Be the person your child can look to, lean on, and learn from.

— JANET PERKINS

ONE DAY AT A TIME

Time has never been something I've worried about. I do what needs to be done when it needs to be done. I don't sit around thinking, *"Maybe I should've done this or that differently,"* because what good does that do? You just keep moving forward, and one day you wake up and realize you've got things you don't even need or want.

That's not how I live. Taking life one day at a time has always worked for me. As I've gotten older, I've leaned into that even more. People ask me why I live like that, and the answer is simple: I believe in the grace of God. I trust that He can work things out, no matter what the situation is.

I've lost some of my best friends over the years—friends who've passed on. But grief? It doesn't linger with me. Oh, I hurt and cry when it happens, of course. But I don't hold on to the grief. If the Lord sees fit to take someone I love, I trust that it's part of His plan. I focus on the good memories, and those memories make me stronger in my faith.

When I think about the people I've lost, I don't get stuck in the sadness. I think about the good times and the laughs we shared. My mother? I laugh out loud sometimes, remembering her. My grandmother? She still makes me smile.

There's no use losing sleep over what you can't change. Sometimes you just have to walk away—understanding that we're all human and we all have to live our own lives. I've never been one to give a lot of advice unless someone asks me. And even then, I can only share my own experiences. I can't tell you how to live your life because I don't know what you've been through.

If I haven't been through it myself, I'll tell you straight up: *"I've never had that experience."* That's where honesty comes in. You don't know everything, and you can't fix everything. Sometimes, the best thing to do is let go and move on. When my time comes, I hope to hear those words: *"Well done, my good and faithful servant."* That's what I strive for. I do my best, and when I hit a rough patch, I either smooth it out or climb over it. But I keep moving forward, always with faith.

One of the greatest lessons my mother ever taught me was this: *"Know yourself. Know who you are and what you want out of life."* She drilled that into me, especially during the civil rights movement. She knew I'd face situations that could be dangerous, and she wanted me to be grounded.

If you don't know yourself, you'll get caught up in someone else's plans and expectations. I've never let that happen. When my father tried to tell me to put my son Glenn up for adoption, I knew better. He said, *"You've got a choice."* But in my heart, I knew I could raise Glenn on my own, whether Leroy accepted it or not.

Doubt? I didn't entertain much of that. I made my decisions, trusted in my ability, and kept moving forward. That's how I've lived my eighty years—trusting that there's someone bigger than me who won't let me fall too far. Oh, I've stumbled, but I've always managed to get back up.

JOY LIKE A RIVER

After eighty years, I can say I've done it all—faced challenges, celebrated milestones, and made peace with the hard parts. My life has been far from perfect, but through it all, I've learned to embrace the journey with faith and gratitude. Most of my life has been good, and for that, I give credit to the grace of God.

As I reflect on the decades behind me, I see not only the milestones but also the smaller, everyday moments that have made life rich and meaningful. Gratitude is not something you stumble upon; it's something you cultivate. I've learned to practice it daily, in both the big things and the little things, and it has shaped the way I see the world.

Life is unpredictable. It throws curveballs, presents challenges, and sometimes feels overwhelming. But in every twist and turn, there has been one practice that grounded me: gratitude. It wasn't something I stumbled upon overnight or mastered in a single moment. Rather, it became a habit I cultivated—a lens through which I chose to see the world. Practicing gratitude every day has changed my life, and I believe it can change yours, too.

Gratitude is about perspective. It's not about pretending life is perfect or ignoring hardships; it's about choosing to focus on the good amidst the bad. Over the years, I've faced my share of challenges. There were times when I didn't know how I'd make ends meet, moments when I lost loved ones who meant the world to me, and days when I felt utterly defeated.

But even in those moments, I found something to be grateful for. Sometimes, it was as simple as the warmth of the sun on my face or the comfort of a kind word from a friend. Gratitude doesn't erase the pain, but it gives you the strength to carry it.

I've learned that when you focus on what you have rather than what you lack, your mindset shifts. You stop dwelling on what's missing and start appreciating what's present. That shift in perspective has been one of the greatest gifts of my life.

I'm looking forward to whatever time I have left. I'm not worried about the future because I know it's not in my hands —it's in God's. What I can do is live the same way I always have: with faith, gratitude, and a little more light around me.

I totally get it—practicing gratitude every day is not easy, especially with the way our world has become. Social media has made it difficult to appreciate what we have or where we are in our own journey. Platforms like Instagram make it even harder, because the moment you log on, you think everyone else has it better than you do—taking multiple vacations a year, perfecting their bodies, buying new homes, getting married, or being proposed to—basically giving you the illusion that these people are living your dream life.

Gratitude doesn't require grand gestures or monumental changes. It's about finding joy in the small things. For me, it might be the aroma of freshly brewed coffee in the morning, the sound of a child's laughter at the diner, or the peace of sitting on the porch watching the world go by.

Gratitude is like a muscle—the more you exercise it, the stronger it becomes. At first, it might feel awkward or forced, especially if you're going through a tough time. But with practice, it becomes second nature.

It takes a lot of faith to stay grateful. Faith has been my anchor, the steady foundation I've stood on through life's storms. From a young age, I was taught to trust in a higher power, and that belief has carried me through every challenge. I've faced financial struggles, the loss of loved ones, and moments of uncertainty, but in those times, I always turned to God.

I've found that faith doesn't mean everything will be easy. It means you trust that things will work out the way they're supposed to, even if you can't see it at the time. There were moments in my life when I didn't know how I would make it through, but I kept praying, kept trusting, and somehow, things always worked out.

Faith isn't just about prayer—it's about action. You can't just ask for help and then sit back and do nothing. You have to get up, do the work, and trust that God will meet you halfway. That's been my approach to life, and it has served me well.

It's easy to be grateful when things are going well, but the real test comes during the hard times. I've had my share of challenges—times when the road was rough and I felt like giving up. But even in those moments, I found reasons to be thankful.

For me, gratitude is deeply connected to my faith. I believe that every blessing, every challenge, and every moment is part of a greater plan. Trusting in that plan has helped me find gratitude even when I didn't understand why certain things were happening.

Faith teaches you to be thankful not just for what you have, but for what you've overcome. It reminds you that even in the darkest moments, there is a light to be found. Practicing gratitude daily is my way of honoring that faith and acknowledging the grace that has carried me through.

When I lost loved ones, the pain was sharp and real, but I chose to focus on the time I had with them rather than the time I'd lost. I'd think about the laughs we shared, the lessons they taught me, and the memories that made me smile. Gratitude doesn't erase the pain, but it gives you a way to carry it with grace.

There were also times when I struggled financially. Those were humbling moments, but they taught me resilience. I learned to appreciate the value of a dollar, the generosity of a neighbor, and the satisfaction of making it through another day. Looking back, I realize those challenges shaped me into a stronger, more compassionate person. For that, I'm grateful.

Life isn't just about challenges—it's also about joy. And

I've had plenty of it. From the simple pleasures of a sunny day to the deep satisfaction of raising my son, I've experienced joy in so many forms.

One of the greatest joys in my life has been family. Raising my son, Glenn, was a journey filled with love, laughter, and lessons. He taught me patience, resilience, and the importance of unconditional love. Watching him grow into the man he is today fills me with pride and gratitude.

Another source of joy has been my community. Over the years, I've been surrounded by people who supported me, encouraged me, and shared life's ups and downs. From neighbors to lifelong friends, these relationships have been a constant source of happiness.

Gratitude doesn't just change your outlook—it changes the way you interact with others. When you practice gratitude, you naturally become more patient, kind, and understanding. You start to see the good in people, even when it's hard to find.

I've noticed that when I express gratitude to others, it creates a ripple effect. A simple "thank you" can brighten someone's day. A genuine compliment can lift their spirits. And when you make a habit of showing appreciation, it encourages others to do the same.

Gratitude strengthens relationships. It reminds you to cherish the people in your life and not take them for granted. Whether it's a spouse, a child, a friend, or a stranger, letting someone know you appreciate them can make a world of difference.

And then there are the little things—like a warm cup of coffee on a cold morning, the sound of birds singing outside my window, or the peace of a quiet evening. These small moments remind me that joy doesn't have to come from big events; it's often found in the everyday.

Loss is a part of life, and I've had my share of it—friends, family members, and even opportunities. All of them have come and gone. But I've learned that loss isn't the end. It's a transition, a reminder that nothing in this world is permanent.

When I think about the people I've lost, I don't dwell on the sadness. Instead, I focus on the joy they brought into my life. My mother, for example, was a strong, wise woman who taught me so much about resilience and love. When I think of her, I smile, remembering her words of wisdom and the laughter we shared.

Loss has also taught me to cherish the present. You never know how much time you have with the people you love, so it's important to make the most of every moment. That's a lesson I carry with me every day.

Start small. Each morning, think of one thing you're thankful for. It could be as simple as waking up to a new day or having a warm meal to eat. Write it down if you can; seeing your blessings on paper can be incredibly powerful.

As you go about your day, look for moments to appreciate. Did someone hold the door open for you? Did a stranger smile at you? Did you accomplish something, no matter how small? These are all opportunities to practice gratitude.

At the end of the day, reflect on what went well. Even if it was a tough day, try to find at least one thing to be thankful for. Over time, you'll start to notice more and more reasons to be grateful.

Every evening, I take a few moments to reflect on my day. I think about the things that made me smile, the people who showed me kindness, and the little victories I achieved. Sometimes the list is long; other times, it's just one or two things. But no matter how small, those moments matter.

I remember something that happened not too long ago—November 27, to be precise. I remember the date because when I got home that day, I wrote it down in my diary. It was the day before Thanksgiving. Glenn and his friend had taken me to the cinema to see *Wicked*. Glenn dropped us off in front of the theater, just across the street from the entrance. As Glenn's friend helped me cross at the zebra crossing, I took my time with my walker, not minding that a little traffic had started to build up while they waited for me to reach the other side.

Then something interesting happened. The young man in the car at the front of the crosswalk called out to Glenn's friend and asked, "Is that your mom?" Glenn's friend said yes. The man then asked, "Are you guys going to eat or something?" We told him we were going to see a movie. He beckoned Glenn's friend over and said, "Listen, man, she just reminds me of my late mom. That's exactly how she used to take her time crossing the road." Then he pulled out his wallet, took out a bill, and handed it to Glenn's friend, saying, "I'm paying for her snacks."

He quickly drove off to make way for the other cars honking behind him. At first, I thought he had given Glenn's friend a five-dollar bill. But when Glenn's friend handed it to me and said, "Here's your snack money," I realized it was a fifty-dollar note. It was the first time something like that had ever happened to me, and I told myself I would write it down in my diary when I got home.

For that young man, it was about being grateful for the beautiful memories he had of his momma and, in his own way, celebrating me for reminding him of her. I still think of him every now and then and wish we'd had enough time to at least get his contact so we could have extended an invitation to our Thanksgiving dinner the next day.

Gratitude is not just a practice—it's a way of life. It's a choice to focus on the good, to appreciate what you have, and to see each day as a gift. No matter where you are in life, it's never too late to start.

So, take a moment today to count your blessings. Look for the good in your life, no matter how small. And as you practice gratitude, watch how it transforms your outlook, your relationships, and your heart. Life is a gift—cherish it, celebrate it, and give thanks for it every day.

At eighty, I know I'm in the final chapters of my life, but that doesn't scare me. In fact, it excites me. I look forward to each new day with curiosity and gratitude, wondering what lessons, joys, or challenges it will bring.

I don't spend much time worrying about the future. Worry doesn't change anything—it only robs you of the present. Instead, I focus on what I can do today: how I can live fully, love deeply, and leave the world a little better than I found it.

Whatever time I have left, I want to spend it in gratitude. Whether it's a quiet morning at home, a phone call with a loved one, or a walk in the sunshine, I want to savor every moment.

When I look back on my life, I see a tapestry of experiences—some beautiful, some painful, but all meaningful. Each moment, each person, and each lesson has contributed to the person I am today.

I've made mistakes, but I've learned from them. I've faced hardships, but I've grown stronger because of them. I've experienced joy, and I've shared it with others. Through it all, I've lived with faith and gratitude—and I wouldn't change a thing.

Life has been a gift, and I'm thankful for every day of it. Whether I have one year left or twenty, I plan to live each day to the fullest, with a heart full of gratitude and a spirit full of light.

Legacy is a funny thing. When someone asked me recently what I thought my legacy would be, I paused—not because I didn't have an answer, but because I wasn't sure how to put it into words. What exactly defines a legacy? Is it the big, bold accomplishments? The titles? The accolades? Or is it the small, quiet ways you live your life—the way you treat people, the lessons you pass on, and the values you embody?

And here's the thing: my legacy isn't finished yet. As much as I've lived and learned, there are still things I want to do, goals I want to achieve, and lessons I want to share. I'm not ready to hang up my hat just yet.

Life is a work in progress, and so is our legacy. Every day is an opportunity to add to it, to refine it, and to make it more meaningful. Whether it's through small acts of kindness, big leaps of faith, or simply showing up as your authentic self, you're building your legacy every single day.

To me, my legacy isn't something flashy or grand. It's simply living as a decent human being. That's it. That's what I've tried to do in my time on this earth—live with integrity, treat people with kindness, and stay true to myself. It's the lessons I've passed on to my son—the importance of faith, hard work, and integrity.

This is the legacy I want to leave behind: a life lived with love, faith, and courage. And when my time comes, I hope those who knew me will remember me not for my achievements or possessions, but for the way I made them feel—loved, valued, and inspired to live their own lives with courage and to find joy in the little triumphs.

ABOUT THE AUTHOR

Janet L. Perkins is a storyteller of resilience whose life embodies the title of her memoir, *Courageous Joy*. Born and raised in Baltimore, she came of age during the turbulence of the civil rights era, being among the very first group of students handpicked to desegregate a public school in Baltimore following *Brown v. Board of Education*.

A devoted mother, Janet raised her son Glenn with fierce love and determination, confronting the challenges of single motherhood and the hard choices required in raising a Black boy in America. Her journey—marked by faith, family, and an unshakable will—reflects the quiet heroism of countless women whose strength often goes unseen.

In addition to her work in government service, where she dedicated decades to the Social Security Administration, Janet has been a lifelong advocate for family, community, and truth-telling. Her story offers not only a personal history but also a window into the broader experiences of Black women who have held families and communities together through courage, sacrifice, and grace.

Now in her later years, Janet writes to ensure that her story—and the lessons within it—lives on for future generations. She believes that remembering is an act of love and that joy, when chosen despite sorrow, is the greatest act of courage.